SEC[RET] HOLLYWOOD SUPER MADAM

SECRETS OF A
HOLLYWOOD
SUPER MADAM

JODY BABYDOL GIBSON

Corona Books and Music
· ·
LOS ANGELES, CALIFORNIA

Published by Corona Books and Music.com

ISBN 13: 978-0-9792202-0-3

ISBN 10: 0-9792202-0-3

Front & Back Cover Concept: Jody Babydol Gibson

Front, Back, and Inside Photos: Jan Sanders

Interior Concept and Layout: Bookcovers.com

This book is dedicated to my sister,
whose strength and courage helped me
survive the darkest journey of my life

Table of Contents

Acknowledgements:

Writing this book was a challenge that I accepted by myself; there was no co-writer or ghost writer. That said, my acknowledgements extend to those who have been there with me along the way...

Thank you Jan Sanders for shooting my lovely cover, Edward L, Anita T, Gary M. for always being there, Mara for her undying support, Z girl for your 'pep talk, Eric R, Emme, "Big Dom E" for being there, Sam & Andy for helping me handle my money, my dear friend Elaine Y may she rest in peace; I know you're watching Elaine, Amy C. for her generous knowledge, Joel G. for helping me mull through the mire, Zeek and the boys for keeping me safe, my mom for keeping my life alive during prison, my daddy for his sense of refinement & the beautiful letters which gave me hope, and my sweetheart Michael for putting up with me & all my madness during the making of this book...

A percentage of the proceeds from this book will go towards a no kill animal rescue.

A percentage of the proceeds from this book will go towards the Denise Brown foundation to help abused women.

Introction

For thirteen years I owned and operated one of the largest and most exclusive Escort services in the world, spanning over 16 states in the US and Europe. While ruling the evenings as the Hollywood Super Madam known only as Sasha, I serviced the sexual secrets of the rich and famous. Employing over 300 girls and catering to over 1000 clients, even Heidi Fleiss had come to work for my service in 1990 before ultimately going out on her own leading to her arrest in 1993. There was no sexual scenario I did not orchestrate or delegate. This gave me an enormous education on men, women, and life that no money could buy. I was prosecuted and convicted in April 2000, and thus sent to the most severe prison in the state of California due to the political agenda surrounding my case as I had no priors or arrests before that. I remained there in Chowchilla for close to 3 years.

This book is about my life servicing the rich and famous… and their sex, sex, sex! From Ben Affleck's steamy night with a hot blonde to Bruce Willis' wild time the champagne flowed. Political figures like Barry Goldwater Jr., as well as House of Representative's Texas Lt. Governor Ben Barnes, baseball legend Tommy La Sorda, and even Supermodel Naomi Campbell's father negotiated with me for a Royal Arab Prince. Their excesses like a week with the richest man in the world The Sultan of Brunei, or the wild parties with Arnold and Sly; from Playboy Playmates to porn stars it's all in here. And the money…find out how one lucky gal got over a million dollars in the country without declaring it!

But it hadn't started like that. The truth was my parents afforded me a wonderful beginning in the affluent suburbs of Westchester, N.Y. I came from a very clean-cut entertainment family with ambitions for a recording career.

The truth is all I really wanted was to make videos for MTV.

My sister was a soap opera star from daytime television, and mom was a personal talent manager famous for discovering a then unknown actor named Thomas Mopather, whose name she changed to Tom Cruise.

See how I moved to Los Angeles with dreams of pop stardom and how it segued to becoming a Hollywood Super Madam. The cat and mouse games of what it took to survive in evading law enforcement for 13 yrs., leading the officer that led the team who managed my capture to comment; "You were my worthiest opponent. If I were doing what you were, I would have done it just like you."

You'll be privy to my girls and their experiences servicing my celebrity clientele as I allow you to eavesdrop in on those very private conversations detailing who had a big dick and who didn't; who was cheap and who was generous, while exposing all their sexual secrets. What were some of the kinky fetishes famous Hollywood producers had? Well, you'll have to read it to believe it!

I share many of my 'tricks of the trade'; the sexual secrets my girls learned that had celebrities and rich men eating out of the palm of their hands. Like the best blowjob ever I affectionately named the Swirly Move as I demonstrated during our sexual education hour one evening in Part Two "Life As a Madam" Chapter 3: Becoming Sasha.

I hold nothing back so you'll excuse me if it gets a little nasty.

See why the men gave my girls all kinds of expensive gifts and how much money they made and what it was like for me to pick up suitcases full of cash!

If you've ever been curious about what it must be like to be a Hollywood Super Madam servicing the rich and famous this is a book you certainly cannot live without.

And finally, read about my hellacious journey through the darkest nights in prison where I saw Satan in the faces of people disguised as women in Part Four "The Conclusion" Chapter 31 Prison; Lesbians, loneliness, violence, and deprivation which will surely show you not to try this at home. I was sent to the most severe prison in the state of California for a so called crime whose only victim was me.

But, I was not a victim- I was a target.

The punishment simply did not fit the crime. And you'll see how the poor conditions of prison life nearly killed me as I lay in a hospital bed fighting for my life.

"Secrets of a Hollywood Super Madam" is the first truly tell all book about surviving it all and for better or worse this was my journey and this is my story...

"They say a person's true wealth is measured by their life experience; if this is true, that would make me a very wealthy woman."

Jody Babydol Gibson

PART ONE:

"What's A Nice Girl Like Me...?"

Chapter 1: Childhood & Puberty

My parents afforded me a wonderful beginning in the affluent suburbs of Westchester County, New York. Mom was a fashion designer then and Dad owned several upscale ladies retail designer boutiques when they met so it was no wonder they initially made a good match. He was the buyer who had impeccable style sense. With his double-breasted jackets complete with matching handkerchief in the chest pocket he really made quite a dashing impression which always reminded me of actor Robert Wagner. Although dad had experienced early fame as a singer on radio when there was no television, and to this day still sounds very much like singer Bing Crosby, it was his sister Georgia Gibbs, my aunt who had gone on to greater fame selling gold records. Aunt Georgia had been Princess Grace's personal choice to sing in Monaco at her wedding to Prince Rainier and she had her very own star on Hollywood Boulevard's Walk of Fame. So, I guess you could say show business was in our family.

Mom would go on to notoriety of her own after her divorce when she would become a talent manager. Her first discovery was an unknown actor named Thomas Mopather, whom she then talked into changing his name to Tom Cruise. She first got the idea to be a talent manager when my sister and I started doing television commercials after being discovered by an agent while we were walking in NYC together. My sister took to acting immediately and landed a lead role on a major soap opera, leading to a long and successful career as a soap opera star. All of these things influenced me early on to decide that what I wanted was to be a recording artist and make videos for MTV.

As a child, mom noticed my ear for music and according to her I couldn't sit still once the music played. At age three she would prop me up on a table when friends came by, put on some music and watch me dance. I would later repeat this when my babysitter Camille would sneak me into the local nightclub at age fourteen. She would watch me show off my dancing skills as I jumped on top of the speakers to perform for the locals there. They would often hear me singing to Billy Holiday songs since blues was my first love as a singer. Dad would coach me and help me with my phrasing. Playing piano tuned my musical tastes and although my early classical training was lovely, I ended up playing what I wanted sounding out the notes by ear.

In school however, I was a bit of a loner who dreamed about the television jobs I was running to NYC to shoot even though what really beckoned me was my love for music. The truth was school came rather easy to me and when I wanted to it was not hard to score an A or B. Besides, my mind was on boys. By the time I was thirteen I had blossomed into a young woman with a bodacious set of natural 38C's. Realizing all the attention this gave me I enjoyed showing them off every chance I could. So, that said, who had time to think about school? With big dreams and greater fish to fry, like most young kids I just couldn't sit still. Even as the Burger King girl in a television commercial I was hired for, I remember sitting next to the girls at school dressed in their Burger King outfits while realizing I was actually filming the television commercial later that day. This gave me perspective which confirmed for me at an early age that I had larger goals than those of my peers. Always dressed in the latest outfits my designer mom insisted on and with the shortest skirts, the other girls were jealous of me. Basically soft spirited with a gentle nature I did not understand why they should be jealous of me and grew to resent them for it. Therefore, I made no effort to get along with them either.

Maybe being an outcast was in my destiny. Or perhaps I was a visionary. Guess it depends on how you look at it.

Things got so bad my parents decided to send me to a posh private school near Bronxville not far from where Bill and Hillary Clinton live. A beautiful school on a lovely estate it offered special courses like Greek Mythology to wealthy kids with no more than ten students per class. I enjoyed cock teasing the male teachers I was off limits to with my tight pants and short skirts. It was truly a blessed idea that my parents had. However, it wouldn't be long before I would get expelled for having sex with my high school sweetheart on the posh school grounds. We were sixteen and he couldn't keep his face out of my pussy. He would spread my lips and work his tongue on my clit for hours making me cum over and over. I guess that was the beginning of my becoming a good little cocksucker too. Even at the tender age of sixteen, I learned how to relax my throat muscles enabling me to take his gorgeous wide cock deep in my throat. My parents were mortified and I was banished from the posh private school forced to return back to the public school with the girls who hated me.

Our beautiful estate in Westchester really showed off dad's artistic side for landscaping and soon became the subject of many sophisticated parties my parents would throw for the network that my sister's soap opera was on. Guests like Superman's Christopher Reeve, Jennifer Aniston's father soap actor John Aniston, and actress Julia Duffy all enjoyed the palatial grounds my father had created complete with a lavish pool and two story private cabanas. I would walk around in the tiniest bikini always strutting my stuff. It was no surprise that I would soon wind up having scandalous affairs often with famous newscasters like Bill Boggs and Chuck Scarborough. Not to mention a brief fling with director Peter Bogdonavich when he picked me out at an open call for dancers while casting his movie "They All Laughed". I was doing my stretches in the corner of a room with what seemed like a thousand other dancers when someone tapped me on the shoulder.

"Hi" the man said.

"Hi" I answered.

"Peter would like to meet you".

"Peter who?"

I was barely eighteen and was not even aware of who was actually directing this film.

"Peter Bogdonovich, the director! Would you like to meet him?" he asked.

"Yeah, okay" I said going along for the ride.

Then, I realized who Peter was. He began to phone me at home as I was still living with my parents. Mom thought that it was for an acting job that would lead to a part in his film. Well, it wasn't exactly for his film. We met privately at the Plaza Hotel in NY. On one occasion after dinner in his room he sang songs to me a cappella. His voice sounded terrible without any music and I was really bored. Then, when he finished what seemed like an hour of singing we got naked. Before I new what happened, he propped my hot, round little eighteen year old ass up in the air and fucked me from be-hind. Although I was barely eighteen and had no idea how to fuck, I sure knew he lasted less than two minutes. He said that he was also seeing an actress in Los Angeles named Dor-othy Stratton.

I guess you could say I was a bit of a wild child.

After graduating high school a decision to 'stray from the tribe' led me to leave home for Europe with a girlfriend and $2000. We were either very stupid or very lucky for immedi-ately we seemed to connect with the European hierarchy there spending our summers on Donald Trump's yacht, then owned by a wealthy Arab arms dealer named Adnan Kashoggi. Little did I know that years later Adnan would be a big client of mine. We partied in Monte Carlo with famed writer Anthony Haden Guest, and dined with "Godfather" screenplay author Lorenzo Semple. Besides basking on the beaches of St. Tro-pez in the south of France we also traveled to Rome where I met director Sergio Leone. Minor modeling jobs like helped finance our trip but we really didn't need much money as the invited guests of such an elite clientele. It was really quite a time. I remained in London for two years before deciding to return home to the United States.

Upon my return, it seemed I was living in the shadows of my well-known manager mother and famous sister. There was no other choice but to leave all that I knew behind and move to Los Angeles to pursue my dreams of pop stardom.

Chapter 2: Becoming Babydol

Arriving in Los Angeles I was completely on my own. I knew no one. After finding a run down apartment in Beverly Hills, and purchasing a used car with $2500 mom had given me before I left it seemed there was much to do. Hard to believe there actually was a run down apartment in Beverly Hills! But it was and at least I was there. No lights, no furniture, just a phone. A cheese burrito was dinner. My family had not been in the record business and so there was no one there to advise me on where to begin.

The first challenge was to support myself. However, the only thing that I knew how to do was to be an agent since I had learned that skill while helping mom answer the phones when she became a talent manager. Opening up a modeling agency was the most natural thing for me to do. So that said, I set up shop in my kitchen, got a cat, had some business cards made, and the Talent Company was born. Realizing the need for client accounts led me to model in most of the shows downtown at the Convention Center wherein, I proceeded to gather accounts for my agency. After one year, there was enough to move forward with. Placing an ad in the trades for models was the next move. Things fell into place and before long I had more models than I knew what to do with.

During this time I met a guy who had a friend in the record business. I begged him to get a meeting for me, which he did. Apparently, Paul Sloman had been an executive with one of the major record companies and had now gone on his own looking for new talent to sign. Paul liked me and asked me if I had a demo for him to hear.

"Of course" I answered.

I really had no idea what a demo was.

"I have to hear how you sound so I can see whether I should sign you" he finished.

"No problem" I said and promised to return with one.

With absolutely no idea where to begin to produce a demo for Paul to hear I wasn't about to let that stop me. While walking down a street in Westwood I stumbled onto an amateur karaoke like recording studio named Recording Star Studio. What were the odds?! I went in to investigate. It seemed that they had a collection of pre-recorded arrangements without vocals on them, and for $12.95 one could actually record three songs. It was a simple four track, with no effects and no "punch-in". This meant that you had one take to sing the entire song. Any mistakes you made remained so what you recorded was what you got. Another take would cost another $12.95. It occurred to me though, that with enough rehearsal I might be able to go for performance value and actually pull off a pretty good demo. I decided to give it a try and recorded three songs, which came out fairly well; the Ben E. King song "Stand By Me", "Tracks Of My Tears", and the theme song "Home" from the Broadway show The Wiz. I still have those original demos.

Two weeks later I met with Paul and gave him my demo. The next day he phoned to inform me of my new production deal with him and asked me which producers I might like to work with. This was pre huge Madonna fame, and singers like Stacey Q and Taylor Dane were making top forty history. I told Paul that blues was where my heart was and he told me that unless I wanted to wind up in Las Vegas as a lounge singer I better learn pop music. He signed me to a contract, which immediately paid my rent. So, ingratiating myself with pop music became my life. Paul knew most of the big record producers and it was easy for him to get me Stacy Q's producer and writer of one of her hit records Willie Wilcox. We began to work daily on these tracks at Willie's house.

On the way home I stopped off at the store to pick up some groceries and caught an ad posted on the wall outside. It was for a talent variety show called "Star Search". Much like today's "American Idol", it featured young amateurs vying for recording industry stardom. I wrote down the information. That night I remembered something Paul had asked me.

"Think about a catchy name; something we might call you" he had said at one of our meetings.

People had nicknamed me "Babydoll" since they said that's how I looked. A light bulb went off in my head! I decided to use the spelling Babydol. It seemed a bit more unusual that way. Thinking about that Star Search audition, I took a chance and sent my photo and new demo tape in as Babydol. I was stunned weeks later when I received the call from the casting director who informed me that I had an audition at Capital Records for the show! That was it. I was Babydol. Immediately I phoned Paul to share the good news. He loved the name and wished me luck for the audition.

Dad worked really hard with me on my song and when the audition came he was thrilled to be by my side and watch his little girl sing. Making it as far as the finals was terribly exciting but alas, having a record deal already in the works disqualified me as I was no longer considered an amateur. Terribly disappointed I returned home to my project with Paul and Willie. Sad at the loss of Star Search, but excited to move forward with finishing up my new album and CD.

Willie and I worked endless hours in his studio to finish the tracks for Paul to get me a major record deal. Quite certain I was on my way, what came next was a complete shock which nearly devastated me. Six months of work in the studio we all felt things were ready. With my finished tracks in hand I ran to get my boom box when I got the call from Paul. He had gotten into a serious car accident and was in the hospital.

"I'll be right over" I said jumping in my car.

I ran to the hospital to see him lying there, conscious, but obviously in really bad condition. I'll never forget what he turned to me and said:

"Sorry, baby. I'm all fucked up. I don't have the use of my legs and they don't know when I'll be able to walk again. I just can't think about your project any more. All that matters to me now is my health."

"Of course," I said while swallowing my heart, "just get better".

This would be one of many setbacks to be encountered in my career in the record business. I went home exhausted and slept in bed for the following three days.

PART TWO:

"Life As A Madam"

Jody Babydol Gibson

Chapter 3: Becoming Sasha

By now business with my modeling agency was booming as I became barraged with accounts. The agency was strictly legitimate and I was very protective of my models. However, I was only making 10% of what my models made which was the standard agent commission. That was barely enough to keep my electricity on! My entertainment background had instilled in me that modeling and acting was no joke. You had to work hard and keep at it if you wanted to succeed. My entrée into the record business had been devastating. But within a few days I came to realize that I must have been doing something right to have gotten signed to a deal my first time out. That inspired me.

It was no coincidence that my models were always asking me if I knew any wealthy sugar daddies to introduce them to, while the wealthy men who were my accounts were always asking me if I knew any pretty models to introduce them to. At first I introduced people to each other out of the goodness of my heart. Then, one day I ran into one of my models driving a brand new Mercedes SL. I commented on what a beautiful car it was and asked her where she got it.

"Wow! Where did you get the nice Benz?"

"From that guy you introduced me to!" she giggled.

"Really? No one even sent me a thank you note!" I re-plied.

Suddenly, it felt like I'd been hit with lightning. It was like an epiphany! I began to wonder how many of these other successful matches I had arranged without knowing it. It appeared that this was really much like being an agent, and that perhaps I should be receiving a fee for all these great introductions. I decided to charge a standard 10% agent fee.

My clients were happy to pay it and before long they started to send their friends. Completely naïve to the world of escorting with my upscale background, I had no idea the standard fee for escort introduction was a 40% cut from each job. Slowly, I began to learn and figure things out. Many mistakes were made and many necessary changes took place. One of which was to use a different name for running an escort service. I couldn't use Jody because of my well-known family ties, and Babydol just didn't seem appropriate. Necessity became the mother of invention and I decided on Sasha. It seemed rather exotic. The agency began to make so much money that in no time, it segued into a full on escort service.

Guess you could say it fell in my lap.

Now as an escort service the money began pouring in. It was time to get back to what I really wanted which was to pursue my recording career. I moved into a big house and got two more cats and two dogs I rescued from the pound. I always tried to rescue them since I was aware of their ill-fated existence in there. Although, we grew up with only two dogs at home, I would soon come to realize my deep love for animals and how precious they all were. There should be a law that determines who can have them since it seemed they were often the victims of those who did not know how to love them.

Soon after, I met a manager named Mike Appel. Well known for discovering Bruce Springsteen and producing the "Born To Run" smash album, Mike and I hit it off immediately and before long he signed me too. Call it a gut feeling, but it seemed better not to mention anything about my extra-curricular activities preferring to let appearances alone and not elaborate on my now thriving escort agency. As far as anyone was concerned I had a legitimate modeling agency. I hadn't begun to write music yet so recognizing the need for songs Mike hired a team of writers to write for me. The tracks were okay but they just didn't grab me. We never seemed to agree creatively and constantly butted heads on most decisions. Partly because I was doing pop music and Mike was truly a Rock n' Roll guy so his taste inevitably gravitated in that direction. My vocals seemed better suited for blues or pop and lacked the raspy, throaty sound that good rock vocals require.

"I think you need to do a remake of 'These Boots Are Made for Walking" he suggested.

"What?!" I said aghast.

I was thinking Janet Jackson and he gave me Nancy Sinatra. Our collaboration lasted a year before I decided it best to move on.

Once again it felt like I'd come close but hit a brick wall. However, I assuaged my emotional wounds by reminding myself that I must have been doing something right for Mike to have signed me. The constant need for songs was a thorn in my side. I needed to either find songs or learn to write. Since most songwriters were saving their best songs for well-known artists who could help further their songwriting careers, I learned how to write songs. Business was booming as my escort empire grew.

Sometimes, I would gather some of the girls together and have a sexual demonstration on the way to orally service men practicing on a dildo;

"Girls, it's important that you understand that the way to his heart is through your blowjob" I would begin.

"Yeah, Sash. Show us!" they cheered eager to know.

"Let's talk about a technique I have affectionately named the "Swirly Move." Once you master this technique your man will think you're a genius! Begin by licking around the head, also known as the helmet. Remember; men love the visual so look up at him while you lick it slowly around the top, and up and down on the shaft like a lollipop. The shaft is his cock. Always be very careful never to use your teeth. Licking him slowly like this will tease him" I began.

"We love to tease" one giggled.

"Now, place one hand around the base of his shaft, and begin to fondle his balls with the other hand, still caressing the outer rim of his helmet with your tongue. He will tell you how to fondle his balls and with how much pressure as this varies from man to man".

"I had one guy tell me to pull on his balls so hard I nearly pulled one right off!" another joked.

"Now, c'mon girls. I'm doing this for your benefit. I already know this stuff" I said.

They were all getting a bit excited.

"Okay, Sash. We'll be good".

"Good. Now, some men enjoy having their balls pulled on aggressively or scratched, while others might prefer a gentler "tickle like" approach. Then, take the head of his cock and placing it in your mouth always mindful of those teeth, slowly begin to move your mouth down towards the base of his shaft where your hand is. He'll love it if you can take the shaft as deep into your throat as possible, which you can do by relaxing your throat muscles. But if you can't take it too deep, having your hand around the base will help you avoid having to take the shaft too deep in your throat without disappointing him" I instructed.

"We never disappoint Sash! There's no money in that!" they all laughed.

I had to calm them down to continue the session. It was important that they know.

"C'mon girls, I'm getting to the best part. Now with the helmet in your mouth, move slowly up and down on the shaft a few times. You should feel him getting turned on as you approach the bottom where your hand is. Keeping his helmet in your mouth, slowly approach the base of his shaft where your hand is. As your hand meets your mouth, on the way up keep them attached to each other, and start turning your hand around in a circular motion to the left just like a hand job. Repeat this slowly, going up and down with him in your mouth, turning your hand around massaging his shaft like a hand job while you suck. Now after you reach the bottom, on your way back up begin to turn your head around in the opposite circular motion of your hand to the right" I instructed again.

It suddenly became so quiet now you could hear a pin drop.

"So, basically are you saying that this will mean your hand is going around in a circular motion to the left, while your head and mouth are moving in an opposite circular motion to the right?" one girl asked.

I knew I had their attention now.

"That's right. Every time your mouth and your hand return to the base of his shaft, begin the circular motion to the left just like a hand job, while your head is swirling around on his cock to the right. You can still fondle his balls with the other hand. You've now mastered the "Swirly Move!" I said.

"Wow, Sash, that's pretty cool!".

They seemed to be enjoying our little sexual demonstration.

"One more thing, girls; remember, you can also increase his arousal by making slurpy like sound effects. They love nasty talk so tell him how much you love to suck his cock, or how beautiful his big cock is which will increase his desire for you. Enthusiasm is the name of the game!" I said.

"I'll say! I'm enthused every time they pull out their wallet!" one girl teased.

I was nearly finished with the demonstration now.

"Precisely. So, if you want to use that "vacuum suck" on the way up by all means do. But, also consider imagining that the inside of your mouth is lined with velvet for that really soft smooth as silk touch. After a few tries, you'll get the rhythm of it. Just remember; hand job in one direction with your head swirling around in the other."

"Ooohh, I love the velvet thing Sash! I never thought of that."

"If you really want to make him yours, gently stick your finger in his ass at the same time while you suck" I finished.

We could sit there playing all night but I had to get back to work. I finished up our demonstration with a quick note on how to perform the Swirly Move while using a condom. But it was worth it since sometimes the prettiest girl could be a complete vegetable in bed.

My casting and agent background in entertainment snatched me a job casting videos for Playboy and Penthouse. This led to my foray into the adult film market. All the Playboy Playmates, Penthouse Pets, and Porn Stars wanted in on my action. Before long, they were swarming to me in droves. Suddenly, I realized that affluent men would pay any price to meet a girl they'd just seen on video or in magazines. And then it hit me;

I was selling fantasy!

It was another epiphany. This new theory, combined with my influx of playmates and porn stars had me sending out photo books daily to clients all over the world at a cost of thousands of dollars. It became clear that what I really needed was a web site to feature them on. The name "California Dreamin' came to mind and my infamous web site was born. I started receiving phone calls from my clients from all over the world telling me they'd never seen anything like this before. Hard to imagine that only fifteen years ago no one had featured photos of models as escorts on the Internet. Technology has come a long way. But back in 1991, no one had thought of it yet so I was the first. This caused my business to quadruple and within three weeks I was earning more money than ever before. I moved into a bigger home and rescued more animals.

MY BABYDOL BILLBOARD
ON SUNSET BLVD.
HOLLYWOOD

Chapter 4: "Who Really Turned In Heidi Fleiss"

"Hi, Sasha. It's Ivan. What are you doing today? Would you go with me to Valentino's on Rodeo Drive? I want to buy a new suit."

That was Ivan all right. We were great friends and spoke on the phone daily about gossip, girls, clients, who was fucking whom, and of course his whacked out relationship with girl-friend Heidi Fleiss. She was a nobody then, a complete un-known. A working $300 escort, she had approached me one year earlier to work for my service. I tried showing her a few things but did not have much luck sending her out… her look simply wasn't right for my clientele. My influx of Playboy Playmates and porn stars had spoiled them. After throwing a few numbers her way to be nice, I gently broke the bad news and sent her on her way. She never forgave me for that.

Few people realize that it was actually Ivan who introduced Heidi Fleiss to the idea of being a madam. He had her steal clients from another well known madam at that time named Alex, whom Ivan had become bitter enemies with. He showed Heidi how to work the phones and deal with girls. Ivan knew how to get the girls, which he did to help her get started. She took to it quickly. He referred to her as a chronic drug user, which I witnessed in her emaciated appearance back then. She enjoyed servicing Columbia drug cartel leaders which is

where most of her big money was made. As I avoided dealing with drugs of any kind, there was certainly no competition
there as I had no use for their business.

Ivan would often confide to me about their sex sessions,
which included him tying her up while he dominated and
abused her physically and mentally. He believed that she was
in love with him. I just didn't understand why. Nor did I care.
I was busy running my escort empire as Sasha, while leading
a public life as Babydol the recording artist. And I had my
hands full at home with a menagerie of now almost 50 animals in my animal shelter. Ivan Nage (pronounced NAHJ) was
an entertaining older guy. A sometime director with credits
like television's "Starsky & Hutch", Ivan had all the right props
to attract the girls: a beautiful boat, Mercedes Benz, a lovely
condo in Century City, and plenty of cocaine to lure them in
with.

"I'll go if you really need me because I'm swamped. I just
finished some new tracks for my new CD."

Ivan was one of the only individuals privy to the truth of
my now "double life" as Sasha/Babydol.

Business had gotten good. Recognizing the need for promotion, I wanted to send press kits to record producers. Afraid
they would steal my ideas, songs, and even my name, I met
with an attorney. He advised me to

"Make the name famous first; then everyone else is a
copy."

Following his good advice, and with business booming, I
managed to snag my own billboard on Sunset Blvd. in the
1 spot at the cost of $35,000 for one month. Shows you
how good business really was because I wrote that check in
a heartbeat! My billboard announced my arrival securing my
identity as Babydol, got me on the news, and was even featured in an extensive layout about Hollywood in National Geo-
graphic Magazine. I was on my way. So, as far as anyone
else was concerned I was Babydol, the recording artist with a
billboard on Sunset.

"Yes, I really need you" Ivan answered.

"Okay, I'm on my way over."

I drove to his condo in Century City with its lovely collection of art.

"Let's go- I'm in a hurry" I said.

And off we went in his white Mercedes Benz. Suddenly, he stopped to pull into a Loves Barbecue, a burgers and ribs joint located on Pico Boulevard in West Los Angeles. I was a vegetarian and he knew that.

"Why are we stopping here?" I inquired curiously.

"I'm just running in to get a cup of coffee." he said.

As we walked in, he seemed to know exactly where he was going and took me with him to join two clean-cut men sitting at a table. He did not introduce me. I thought that seemed odd, too. After a moment the conversation began. I heard Ivan use words like bank account, along with their account numbers, locations of deposits, routing patterns.

"This is the information on Heidi. This is where her bank account is. This is where she does the money laundering" I heard him say.

And then it hit me; Ivan was giving up Heidi's bank accounts to these two men! But, who were they? And what was I doing here? And better yet, who did they think I was?! Suddenly, their identities became clearer. One was an agent with the IRS, and the other was a detective in the elite section of Bunko at the Beverly Hills Police department. I knew well that Bunko was for credit card theft and fraud. The two men were writing all this down. Apparently, this detective was piecing a fraudulent credit card case together against Heidi. I couldn't help but notice him staring at me and thinking he was really cute in a Tom Cruise kind of way. But I was witnessing Ivan giving Heidi up to the cops! Why was Ivan placing me at risk by dragging me along? I began to feel very nervous with the whole scene wondering if it showed on my face. I felt trapped. Obviously, I couldn't just get up and leave as that would make me look suspicious. Were 20 cops about to bust their way in now and arrest me next? My heart was pounding so loud I was certain they could hear it. I remembered that my Babydol billboard was dominating Sunset Blvd. just a few blocks away. So, if anyone asked, I was a recording artist. I sat there listening to it all quietly and motionless. The handsome detective was flirting with me and trying to get my attention. But, at that moment all I could think about was what would happen next.

The meeting lasted about an hour but it seemed like forever until it was finally over. I kept thinking that at any moment the police were coming to take me away in handcuffs but that didn't happen. Not that day anyway. The detective shot me a sexy look one more time and gave me his card as both men got up to leave. I remained there seated next to Ivan. After getting up enough strength, I turned to him and asked

"Ivan, why did you do that to Heidi?"

"I had to get her before she got me" was all he said.

Apparently, I learned later on that he had become bitter over her rejection of him once she had gotten successful. It seemed she had cut him out and he was mad. Still taken aback by it all we left and made our way over to Valentinos to buy him that suit. Eventually, I realized that I was numb but all right. And also, I just couldn't get that detective out of my mind...

Chapter 5: "Receiving Immunity-Love Finds A Detective"

The arrest of Heidi Fleiss made headlines around the world in 1993. I still remember it as if it were yesterday. If you would have told me that the same gal who had looked so sickly when she came to work for my service as an escort two years before would now make headlines around the world as a famous madam, I would have told you that you were crazy! I wanted to phone Ivan but couldn't. At the insistence of my detective, now my lover, I had severed my ties with Ivan. Apparently, that fateful meeting between the IRS agent and my detective had panned out after all leading to Heidi's arrest. Day after day I watched it play out with growing fascination. It wasn't long before I received a very disturbing phone call. It was from my detective.

"You're next" he said.

"What do you mean?!" I asked in a panic.

"They know all about you, so it's just a matter of time" he offered.

"What now? What should I do?"

"I don't know. Let me see and I'll phone you tomorrow" he said calmly.

Jody Babydol Gibson

My life began to flash before me. I started to think about how he and I had met after that fated meeting with Ivan at the Loves Barbeque. Unable to resist the temptation any longer I decided seven months earlier, and quite a few weeks after that first meeting with Ivan, that perhaps I should give him a call. He was handsome and it wouldn't hurt to have a detective in my life.

On our first date we met during the day at a coffee shop. We clicked right away and it was love at first sight. We began seeing each other all the time. He used to love to have me drive around with him in his unmarked detective car and sometimes he'd even put the siren on for fun.

Every now and then, my detective would sneak me upstairs in the police department to his office in the elite Bunko section. One day, I overheard a conversation between the other detectives. They were discussing the business of a successful growing madam in town named Sasha. They were talking about me! Listening intently, I found out they actually knew very little. My efforts of disguise had served me well for they had no clue as to what I looked like or where I lived. Nothing about the dark blue Mercedes Benz I drove either. All they knew was the name Sasha, and that she was doing increasingly well. I decided it best to keep it a secret from my detective lover a while longer.

He loved showing me off and having me around. We began to have sex all over the Beverly Hills Police Department. I sucked his cock in the stairwell, on the roof, and in their gym. It had a television and some nice gym equipment. I loved sucking his cock in that stairwell. Kinky sex like that got him off, too. He loved all our naughty sessions there which got me more excited. I think he liked it best when it was sneaky and dangerous.

We were getting really close and I knew that it was just a matter of time before I would have to reveal myself to him as Sasha, the notorious madam. I wondered how he would take it. Would he get angry with me for keeping it from me? Would he think I was a deceptive liar? Or would he think it was all deliciously decadent and be fascinated by the whole

42

thing?! I concealed my double life from him as long as I could. With my billboard on Sunset, and the tracks I played for him that I was recording, there was no reason for him to think anything other than that of me as a recording artist.

And then, it happened. It was on the night of my birthday. He took me out to a lovely romantic dinner to a restaurant nestled amongst some trees. Sitting there, staring at him while he ate he looked so handsome to me. We kissed a lot during dinner and had a wonderful time. When the waiter asked if we were having dessert he whispered in my ear

"I'm having you for dessert."

We got back into his car. I remember what I was wearing. It was a long, slinky black, body hugging dress like something Morticia would have worn in the Addams Family. Without much notice he abruptly grabbed my tight dress, and lifting it high towards my chest slipped his finger to pull aside my g-string panty and began to eat my pussy. I always enjoyed the feel of his lips and tongue licking me, licking my clit, eager not to miss a drop. He could really make me cum. When he was finished making me cum several times I reached to pull down my dress.

I noticed it was 11 0'clock. Suddenly, I remembered I had booked a big job that night and needed to see how things were going. Almost in the same instant my pager began to go off over and over, as if one of the girls was frantically trying to reach me. He shot me a puzzled look which disturbed me. I didn't want to lose him but clearly, I had to say something. I figured that since he was sitting there with the juice from my pussy all over his lips this was as good a time as any.

"Why is your pager going off over and over at 11 o'clock at night?! Are you seeing somebody else?" he asked.

"Babe, I have something to tell you" I began nervously.

He just sat there looking at me without saying a word.

"You know that madam you keep hearing all those things about named Sasha? Well, you're looking at her!"

There. It was out. I waited for his reaction. He said nothing. I began to elaborate by telling him all about how I'd been living this double life as Sash/Babydol, with all the clients and all the girls. I told him about how afraid I was that they were coming to get me next. He looked at me and said

"You did all that? All by yourself?! That's amazing!"

He found my whole story fascinating, impressed that I had been able to keep it all together. I told him about how Heidi had tried to set me up during an investigation and how I'd narrowly escaped. This infuriated him.

"That bitch won't be around much longer to bother you again" he promised.

Suddenly, I felt safe knowing that he was going to protect me. I was so relieved that he didn't hate me. He dropped me off that night and I realized I had made one of the best friends I would ever have…

And he was right. She had been arrested and it had all come down to this. I snapped back to reality as I realized we were hanging up the phone.

"Just sit tight. Don't speak to anyone until I talk to you to-morrow" he demanded.

"Okay. I love you. Call me tomorrow" I said.

"I love you too."

It's hard to believe I got any sleep at all that night. A million thoughts ran through my head. What was he going to do? What could he do? I knew that he was intent on saving me but now he'd really be putting his job on the line. Would he really be able to do something for me in my desperate hour of need? I thought about the possibility of going to prison and was certain I could never survive that. This was going to be a long night.

It seemed like forever until he phoned which was actually before noon the next morning.

"I've worked something out for you" he began.

"Really? What?" I asked.

He began to explain that his partner had actually been the head investigating officer on the arrest of Heidi Fleiss. He felt

44

that we should speak in person so we made a time to meet that afternoon over at the coffee shop where we had first met on Santa Monica Boulevard in West Hollywood.

I was so glad to see him and wrapped my arms around him afraid to let him go. When I finally did, we went inside and sat down at a table.

"I've worked out a way for you to receive immunity" he said.

"What? How? What do I have to do?" I asked certain that there must be a catch.

I'd always heard that you get immunity when you turn people in and I wasn't about to do that.

"I'm not going to talk" I said.

"All you have to do is meet with the Prosecuting Attorney on the case and tell him who you are. It's just a formality."

"A formality? You're asking me to confess to the Prosecuting Attorney?!"

"Yes, but nothing's going to happen to you, babe. You're gonna' walk" he promised.

"How do I know that for sure? What if this is all a trap?" I asked.

"It's not. But you're just going to have to trust me" he said.

"I'm not signing anything and I'm not talking about anybody else" I instructed.

He could see how serious I was.

"Okay. Just tell them about you and promise you won't do it again. I'll be there, and my partner Sammy will be there, and so will Alan Turner the Prosecuting Attorney. That's it."

I had no idea what to think or say. Figuring I really had no choice at this point, I reluctantly agreed. We kissed and he whispered

"Don't worry. I'll be there to protect you and make sure nothing happens to you."

Call it gut instinct, but for some reason I believed him.

The meeting was set for the following Tuesday afternoon. I had several days in between to think and so I began to formulate a plan. One of my attorneys was a pro-temp judge in Beverly Hills. Since there would be no paper I agreed to sign verifying this immunity, I felt that perhaps I should have someone there as a witness. I went in to talk to my attorney. His name was Richard Green and he was well respected in Beverly Hills. I began to tell Richard my whole story about how I was having this love affair with the detective, and how he had made a promise to get me immunity, and what they were expecting me to do.

"Richard, I need you there with me to witness this. Otherwise, someone could turn around a year later and say it never happened" I began.

"Tell me you're kidding, Sash" he said.

He looked at me with one of those 'Oh brother, what have you gotten me into' looks. But, he agreed to go with me to the meeting.

Tuesday afternoon finally came. Seated there were my attorney Richard, the Prosecuting Attorney Alan Turner, my detective lover, his partner Sammy, and the head of the Organized Crime Task Force. My detective lover introduced me as Babydol, the recording artist. With my attorney seated to my right, I began to explain that I had been the notorious Madam Sasha. They actually seemed fascinated as they questioned me about my operation. How did I find my clients? Where did I get the girls? I was careful to sound like I was saying a lot, but really said nothing. Always mindful to avoid being trapped and never mentioned anything about anyone else, just myself. I was terrified and had no idea what to expect next. My detective lover shot me a loving look as if to let me know everything was going to be okay. After I was finished, the prosecuting attorney began to speak.

"Miss Gibson" he began sternly. "You've complied by coming in to discuss with us what you did. We are going to let you walk. But don't ever let me find out about you operating in this town again" he instructed.

Whew! It was over! Quietly, I smiled over at my lover, and promised I never would operate in this town again.

And then, I walked out and opened up sixteen offices all over the United States and Europe...

PART THREE

"The Names" Pt 1

*A*ll of the client names presented herein were used as public record during my trial to aid in my prosecution and conviction. These names will include actual data from my trial marked as "exhibit # ". They are stamped with the official court seal taken from the Superior Criminal Court in Los Angeles, California determining their authenticity.

You will see three sources of data retrieved from my personal belongings by law enforcement. They will include;

a) My actual "Black Book" #1 with appointments, names, and dollar amounts

b) My actual "Black Book" #2 with names, addresses, and phone numbers

c) The printout from my portable Wizard with names and phone numbers

Chapter 6: Ben Affleck

I was enjoying a lovely spring day on the deck of my friend's boat out on Lake Havasu, Arizona, when my pager suddenly went off. There were no holidays, no vacations. Not when it came to the phone. Calls meant money and I always made it a point to never miss a call. Phoning in to retrieve the message left on my pager was the only way for clients and girls to reach me. I had set things up as one of the many ways and buffers used to avoid being contacted directly to avert an attempt to set me up or worse tape me on the phone. During my thirteen-year reign as the Hollywood Super Madam, I created many ways to insure my safety, which included no direct phone calls from anyone. Everyone, and I mean everyone, had to leave a message. This offered me an opportunity to decide whether or not to return the call in case something sounded suspicious as sometimes it did. It also gave me a heads-up on who might be trying to reach me. My 800# number was listed on my now infamous web site "California Dreamin'" used to display photos of available escorts employed with my service. Changing the photos weekly I opted to keep things simple by offering only forty or so models on the site. Too many choices ultimately confused men sometimes making them unable to choose at all.

When I checked my pager there was a handsome voice on the other end.

"Hi, it's Ben. Call me."

He left his room number at the Beverly Hills Hotel in Beverly Hills. I was pleasantly surprised but somewhat taken aback when I returned the call. A hotel operator answered and demanded

"Who shall I say is calling for Mr. Affleck?"

I became a bit startled and hung up. There would be a lot of talk around town soon after that Ben Affleck and Tom Sizemore were paying to see girls during the making of the movie they filmed together Pearl Harbor. I actually had two girls employed with my service who had seen Tom. One had been paid $800 from Tom Sizemore and according to her, when in his company most of what he did was run his films to show off his movies. But until now I had not had either as a client. Now, it seemed that Ben Affleck was phoning my service for a girl.

As my web site held a secret password known only to my clients it was impossible to locate it by doing an online search for escorts, call girls, or any keywords that might lead one to the privacy of my site. I only dealt by referral; which meant you had to be referred by someone who knew me and it had to be verified by that referred individual, or you didn't get to do business with my service.

Apparently, Mr. Affleck had been referred by someone who knew me. Sheer curiosity would have made it impossible to ignore and so I returned the call. When the hotel operator answered this time I gave her the room number Ben had left for me. She then asked who was calling and after answering "Sasha" I was put through to his room.

"Hi, Ben. This is Sasha returning your call."

"Oh, hi...are you the one in #12?" he asked.

"I beg your pardon?"

"The pretty blonde with the long hair. #12, is that really you?"

Apparently, Ben thought he was contacting one of the girls featured on my site directly.

"No, Ben. I'm the owner of the site, Sasha. But if #12 is the one you like, there is no problem in meeting her" I explained.

"Yes. She's the one I'm trying to reach" he confirmed.

"No problem. Tell me, who referred you to my site?"

I was anxious to know who had referred Ben Affleck to me... although he had me at "hello"!

Ben mentioned the appropriate name, which I later verified when we got off the phone. But for now, our conversation continued.

"So, is that who you'd like for this evening, Ben? Have you had a chance to peruse my web site and did you see anyone else there that you liked?" I inquired.

I was trying to sound a bit playful to break the ice. After all I was used to having celebrities and the rich and famous call me so it was business as usual.

"Yes I have. Looks like you've got quite a selection there" he added playfully.

"Thanks, we aim to please" I played right back.

"Well, I am partial to a gal with a pretty face. Who's the one in# 8?" he inquired.

"Oh, that's Sarah. She's a real sweetheart but I'm afraid she's out of town on a modeling shoot. The gal you first thought you were contacting is Alyssa # 12. She's a real doll."

He went on to say that his preference for that evening was for a busty blonde, 5' 6"- 5' 9 ", with long hair, and made it clear he wanted someone with an upbeat personality. He stated that it was likely he might keep her the whole night.

"No problem" I answered.

The two most important words in the English language were always 'no problem'.

"She's 5' 8", a 38D, long blonde hair, great figure, well dressed, gorgeous, and oodles of fun!

"I'm sure you'll really have a great time with her" I suggested.

"Looks pretty hot" he agreed as he briefly began to view the other available photos online.

"Anything in particular she should wear or perhaps bring?" I inquired.

This was a standard question to all clients as it immediately opened the door and offered them an opportunity to tell me whatever else they might desire sexually or otherwise which could include anything from toys, to the addition of another girl for a possible threesome scenario. Boy, would I love to hear your fantasies, Ben! I was hoping he'd go into a big speech about a particular sexual fetish he was harboring but alas, Ben was quite the gentleman so far on the phone.

"Just have her dressed in a hot two piece suit since she needs to come here to the hotel, and maybe with some sexy lingerie too. Oh, and make sure she wears a short skirt. I like long legs in high heels. Does she party?" he asked.

"Yes, I'm sure she does however, you're on your own there my friend" I answered somewhat firmly.

We both knew what that meant. Likely, he wanted someone who could join him in drink and drugs. This was pre J.Lo and Ben was single then and quite the partier. It was no secret that he had been in and out of rehabs. My policy was never to supply the "party favors" so my answer made it clear that you could party if you wanted to, but you would have to find a way to locate it yourself. No matter who the client was, celebrity, CEO or king, or how much money they spent.... this steadfast refusal to supply drugs saved me from an additional drug related charge during my trial.

"Got it, Sasha. So, how much?" Ben asked.

"Well, that would depend on how long you keep her" I answered.

"Aaaah, makes sense. What about for the whole night?" he asked.

"$3500 for the night or you can keep her a couple of hours for $1500" I answered.

Often my prices ran higher at $1000 per hour, and up to $5000 to $10,000 for the entire night. But after all, this was Ben Affleck.

"I don't think a few hours is gonna do it for me tonight, Sasha. I really need to relax. Cash okay?" he asked.

"Always accepted here" I joked.

The truth was I only accepted cash as I felt a trail of credit cards or personal checks placed me in jeopardy for an un-wanted money laundering charge. Cash flow was harder to prove. But, there seemed to be no need for that speech now.

"Excellent. Her name's Alyssa, huh? Have Alyssa here at 8 PM. I'm in Bungalow # 6. She may need to be announced so I'll leave her name" Ben said.

The private bungalows were located in a more remote sec-tion of the hotel. You could get there by cutting across the grass on the side, and bypass entering through the front if you knew your way but security might still stop you. My girls would be wearing high heels too, so they would be entering the hotel through the front lobby.

"No problem. I know the drill. You'll have a great time. Talk to you later" I answered and hung up the phone.

My next call was to Alyssa. I already had four other girls that looked like her in mind in case she was unavailable. You always needed back up in this business since girls get their period, had boyfriend problems, drama, so on and so forth. Alyssa answered the phone.

"Hello?" a sweet voice said.

"Hey, gorgeous, it's Sash. Are you available tonight?" I started.

"Sure, what's up?" she asked

Alyssa rarely refused a good gig. I liked that she was reli-able and responsible with the money, which are two recipes for success in the escort arena. A girl that was punctual, as well as responsible when it came to handling the money with clients, and getting it to me on time was worth her weight in gold.

"Are you sitting down?" I teased.

"Oooh, this sounds interesting. Yes, I am" she answered.

"Well, girl, you've got a date tonight and it's with Ben Affleck!" I said.

"Wow! No way! How did you get him?!" she snickered.

"I have my ways" I teased.

Even though I had really good relationships with the girls it wasn't my style to ever reveal too much information about any of my business practices.

"Now, let's chat about what you're going to wear. He saw your pic and thought you looked hot and suggested you show up in a hot two piece short skirt suit and heels with some sexy lingerie underneath" I said.

This was one of those moments in which what Alyssa wore and how she looked would immediately determine whether or not she would get to spend the night with Ben Affleck. After all, if he expected a classy, beautiful blonde in a hot short skirt suit with high heels and lingerie, than it was my job to make sure that's exactly what he got.

"Remember that stunning burgundy, short suit you purchased with that client in Italy last year? It looked smashing on you and fit real well" I suggested.

As men could rarely tell the difference between a Chanel suit or a knock-off from Target, it was more important that what a gal wore fit her and looked well on her, rather than what designer duds she had on. A smart classic, well-fitted suit that showed off her long legs and was elegant in its simplicity would speak volumes.

"Yes, I just picked it up from the cleaners. You think I should wear that one?" she asked.

"Absolutely. And he wants you to have on some sexy lingerie underneath so pull out those La Perla sets!" I laughed.

The girls were always well stocked on lingerie at my insistence as it was a pretty standard request from clients. My Agency Rules demanded that bras and panties must match.

"Hey, girl, don't forget your candles!" I reminded her.

"Oooh, you're right! He'll love that! "she said.

I suggested the girls bring some candles to create good lighting to set the scene.

"He sounds like he's in a real party mood. Might keep you up the whole night" I offered.

"Cool. Sounds like a hot gig, Sash! How much?" she inquired.

Alyssa was quite familiar with my high prices as she was one of my most sought after girls.

"I gave him a deal. Hope you don't mind. $3500 for the night; $1500 if he only keeps you for a couple of hours. But, if I know you, you'll be staying the whole night you lucky girl!" we laughed.

"Boy, you sure did give him a deal, huh? But, what the heck- he's a hottie!" she answered.

"Alyssa, he indicated he wanted to party so you know you're on your own with that." I said.

"No problem, Sash. I know just what to do" she assured me.

She was familiar with my business policies, but smart enough to read between the lines knowing well that the longer she stayed the more money she'd make.

"Hey, what time?" she asked.

"8 PM at the Beverly Hills Hotel in bungalow # 6. Don't try to avoid security by entering directly on the side of the hotel on Benedict Canyon. He will be leaving your name there so don't worry if they insist that you be escorted."

This was a common practice among the rich and famous staying in hotels as it afforded them added privacy. If one was located in a private section of the hotel not accessible to the public, one might need to be announced and privately escorted by security to gain entry. Alyssa was more than familiar with this sort of scenario having gone to lavish hotels on my jobs many times before.

"Got it. I just got this awesome new bra and panty set I'm sure he'll love. Maybe I'll wear it with some sexy thigh-high stockings. What about toys? Does he want that too?" she inquired.

"Well, wouldn't hurt. I'd bring a small overnight bag. Wouldn't want security stopping to escort you and see you with a bag full of dildos and lube! Oh, and don't forget to bring condoms" I teased as we both enjoyed a good laugh.

That would be the one rule out of my two page Agency Rules all the girls received upon meeting me that would get me convicted during my high profile trial years later. But I felt it was an important factor as men sometimes forgot to bring them. Having the girls read an outline of my Agency Rules helped conserve my voice from getting hoarse during hours of interviewing new girls and it answered many of their questions.

"Listen, call me and check in when you get there" I continued.

"Got it. Hey, did he happen to mention anything else he might be into?"

"No, but he looks like quite the stud man to me!" I joked.

"Yeah, he sure does! I wonder if he has a big cock?!

"I have no idea but I'm sure you'll let me know." I added.

" Oh yeah, I bet he does and I sure will. Well, Ok, Sash, I'll talk to you later" Alyssa said as we hung up the phone.

I went on with the rest of my afternoon thinking about how much fun she would have with a hot celebrity like Ben Affleck. Even though my business seemed glamorous to most, much of the time it was the girls who were the ones that had all the fun while it seemed all I did was work the phones.

Returning to my post outside I went and took a seat on the deck of the boat with my phone and pager by my side like my two best friends. I had many phones and pagers in those days as technology was a bit less sophisticated back then. One cell phone was for calls to Europe, one for domestic calls, and one for when I was out on the water as many phones did not have good reception out there. In addition there were three pagers; one for the girls, one for clients and my 800# pager from my web site. I also had a little gizmo for use on pay phones that one of the girls had brought me back from Hong Kong. Quite tiny, it held the capacity to sound exactly like quarters one would insert into the phone. All I had to do was hold it up near the earpiece and press, and it replicated the sound of as much change as needed enabling me to phone all over the world for free! I whacked out many pay phones for thousands of dollars of free calls in those days. Sometimes pay phones were the safest way to do business when evading the watchful eye of law enforcement. The rest of the evening remained quiet.

Later that evening Alyssa phoned to tell me she had arrived at Ben's private bungalow and that everything was fine. I did not here back from her again until three in the afternoon of the following day.

"Hey, Sash, it's Alyssa. Call me."

She sounded exhausted.

The girls knew I always required all the juicy details sexually and otherwise that took place with a client. It was essential in determining who to send him the next time. And there was almost always a next time. A common practice that the girls were familiar with, I insisted they call me after each appointment so I may know the details of every sexual encounter. It was important that I be fully informed on exactly what each client requested, whatever little nuances or special things he liked. His sexual preferences which might include his favorite sexual position, or even how he liked his cock sucked, everything he desired which perhaps he might not have included in his conversations with me. I was pretty thorough in my approach with clients and made them feel relaxed and comfortable about telling me anything and I mean anything. So, there were few surprises but I still insisted on it and enjoyed hearing about all the sex too.

I picked up the phone to return Alyssa's page.

"Hi, girl, how'd it go? You sound absolutely exhausted!" I began.

"Oh, I am but he was soooo hot! Oh, My God, he gave it to me all night!" she exclaimed.

"Really? Do tell. How big was he? Which way did he like fucking you the most?" I said with a twinge of jealousy in a fun sort of way like girls do.

"Sash, he's like a good eight inches! Plus, after doing coke all night it seemed like he could stay hard forever! He liked me on all fours of course with my ass up in the air. But my favorite was sitting on him 'cause he was so cute to look at." she said.

My mind began to wander as I imagined a hot looking guy like Ben, with his big, fat, rock hard dick. How sexy that must've been to enjoy feeling him enter inside, filling her up with his warm cock in her ready, wet pussy.

"Sash, are you listening?" she interrupted my thoughts.

"Mmmm, sounds yummy" I commented.

I was getting real wet.

"How was the bungalow? Was it gorgeous?" I asked.

After all, the girls were the ones who got to go on all those shopping sprees, lavish dinners, and have steamy sex with hot celebrities while all I ever did it was put the deals together. But alas, there are worse ways to get off and admittedly, I did live vicariously through their experiences.

"Yeah, he was such a great fuck!" Alyssa admitted.

Now I was really getting hot.

"We began in the Jacuzzi he had in his room. He loved my titties and went crazy sucking on them while they were all wet. I sucked his cock in there first. Remember that session you and I had once where you demonstrated on a dildo how to lick a guy's balls and take his cock deep in my throat while sticking my finger up his ass? Well, it worked! Then, we jumped out and he fucked me right there on the floor! Of course I quickly opted for the comfort of the big bed in the room. The rug burns on both my elbows are killing me! We stayed up all night doing coke. And of course, money was no object so you know I ordered some of my favorite Crystal champagne! It was the best gig I ever had!" she exclaimed again. "Plus" she continued, "Not only did he have a great cock, but he sure knew how to use it! He had this way of fucking me where he would pound me real fast for a while then slow down almost like teasing me, and then give it to me hard again. I'm a wreck! I probably won't walk for a week! I know how you avoid getting involved with supplying any of the party favors. I had a friend on standby with the coke for us so we wouldn't run out" she said.

"Good thinking girl. So, how much did you end up getting?" I asked.

It was back to business and she knew quite that well I meant how much money.

"Well, he gave me the $3500 for the night, plus he tipped me $500" she admitted.

I noted the tip in his file. The girls knew my policy on tips was that they could keep all gifts and tips for themselves; as I always felt if they got it- likely they earned it so, they always told me the truth. If they were lovely company enough to receive something extra from a client, then they should keep it. Most other services however did take 50% of their tips.

"Great! Why don't you get some sleep now and call me tomorrow and we'll settle up then" I suggested.

"Okay, I'm sure I'll sleep 'till tomorrow" she laughed. "Thanks, Sash. Talk to you later."

"No problem. Bye."

I was sure we'd be chatting about this again and probably for a long time...

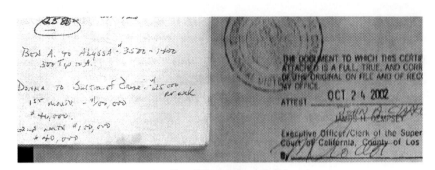

Chapter 7: Sly, Arnold, Robert Horry and VIP Planet Hollywood

I supplied the sex and debauchery to many of the VIP Planet Hollywood parties during one or more of their grand openings. In those days, the restaurants were doing well as they began to pop up all over. It was 4th of July weekend when I received the call from rock star Alice Cooper's manager Shep Gordon. Shep was a soft-spoken darling guy that was now one of their investors. He lived on a beautiful estate in Beverly Hills which featured a sign on the lawn that read; "Alice doesn't live here anymore."

"Hey, Sash, know who this is?" he began.

My keen law enforcement survival techniques along with my years of audio in the recording studio producing my CDs for my then recording career had made me quite good at determining a lot just from hearing a voice on the phone.

"Of course I do, silly. How goes it?" I asked teasing in slang. Clearly, I knew it was Shep.

"Well, we're opening another restaurant in Maui, Hawaii this weekend" he said.

"Congratulations! Nice to see them doing so well" I replied.

"Thanks. This one will really be a blast! Major red carpet affair followed by a big VIP party afterwards in beautiful Maui, Hawaii! The guest list includes Sly Stallone, Arnold Schwarzenegger, Mike Myers, Melanie Griffith, NBA player Robert Horry, and a bunch of others. How say you grab a few of your hotties and fly out here to make the opening?" he asked.

He meant Arnold, as in Schwarzeneggar. This was pre-Governor of California and he was just a movie star back then.

"Mmmm, well I'm not sure I can get away this weekend. I've got a lot going on" I said.

"Sash, c'mon! it'll be fun! Let me tear you away from that damn phone for a couple of days!"

"Well, what's the plan?" I inquired.

The reality of this moment threw my thinking into a bit of a spin since I had been leading two separate lives: One, as Babydol the recording artist; and another maintaining my alter ego Sasha, ruler of the Escort Empire. I had gone to great pains certainly with my high profile record industry clients to keep these two lives separate which was sometimes the hardest thing to do. Especially after completing a great recording project I'd be just dying for them to listen to. But, I was also well aware that those who knew me as the ruthless Super Madam Sasha would never believe that I could also be the light, upbeat, pop star Babydol. Their knowledge of this would have completely undermined my talents in my recording career. So, it was quite rare for me to ever make an appearance as Sasha with my clients and only did so when meeting the girls.

"The plan is I fly you and three of your hottest girls here to Maui, put you up in a gorgeous hotel, and you all join me to dinner with Sly, Arnold, and Melanie Griffith. Then we party the night away at the VIP party afterward" Shep suggested.

"Sounds like fun. It's a long flight to make for one night though."

I reminded him that the flight from Los Angeles to Maui was six hours.

"Ok, then. How 'bout I put you all up for two nights and pay the girls $4000 each. They can do what they want for the second night since I only need them there for the first night red carpet grand opening. Sash, please? I really need you on this one" he begged.

I had to do some quick thinking to come up with an answer here. He was a good client and the offer was irresistible. But, I was most uncompromising when it came to letting clients meet me as Sasha especially since he was a high profile person in the record business.

"I have an idea" I offered. "I'll send my niece Babydol, the recording artist. She'll follow my instructions and look after the girls and this way I won't have to tear myself away from work this weekend. Plus she looks real good."

I laughed quietly realizing he'd never know since he'd never seen me in person.

"Ok, that'll work. You sure she knows what she's doing? I'd feel a lot better if you were there" he said.

"Nah, it'll be just fine. She'll know exactly how to handle everything" I assured him.

I realized that this way my anonymity as Sasha would be secured.

Actually, at that moment I felt rather pleased with the idea. I could party the night away as Babydol amongst the VIPs, which was where I wanted to be anyway, while handling all the business and making the money silently as Sasha the Super Madam! And since I was always pumping the money into my recording career which frequently ran over budget, there was always the need for the business of making money. A perfect solution! I'd make up some story to the girls as to why my name for the night was Babydol. But I knew they probably wouldn't care or pick up on it anyway as they'd be preoccupied with themselves. It was always interesting to me that even with my face perched high atop Sunset Blvd on a massive billboard promoting my recording career, somehow the girls in my service never put it together that I was both Sasha and Babydol and never asked.

"Ok, then. Get back to me with the specifics as soon as you can" he added.

"Alright. I'll phone your assistant with the names for the tickets" I answered.

Amazing to think that to this day and with much of my moving around between keeping my then animal shelter with up to 50 animals from Animal Control, (they always complained that I had too many) evading law enforcement, and going through years of incarceration after my conviction, I still somehow managed to hang on to those airplane ticket boarding pass stubs with our names on them!

"Cool. Thanks, Sash. Your gorgeous gals will really make the place look good. Just one thing" he added.

"What?" I inquired.

"I'll pay her and she'll pay the girls. Make sure your girls understand they have to make themselves available to Sly and Arnold."

"No problem. I understand" I said.

Like they would really argue with that!

"Let me run now and get to work since you're not giving me much time and it's a holiday weekend. I'll phone you back" I finished.

"Ok, Sash. Bye" he said as we hung up the phone.

I immediately decided on a beautiful brunette Porn Star named Jennifer for Arnold since I had remembered my friend Jill's experience with him on the set during a film. Jill was his hot looking brunette, make up artist on one of his films. She had told me how he chased her around on the set all day. So, I had an idea of what type he liked.

The other two gals I phoned were a famous Playboy Playmate, and a tall model, since I knew Stallone had a thing for models. It was no secret that in those days Sly would actually take a hotel room and have Madams and others send him models all day long, which he would parade in and out of the hotel until he found the one he wanted. Now, he was divorced from Brigitte Nielsen whom I had no idea I would meet years later when she would approach me with a request to meet wealthy Arab sheiks. I guess she went through whatever monies she had received from her divorce from Sly. The Arab princes paid big money for high profile American actresses that they recognized from magazines or television and practically had an obsession with them.

Surprisingly, all three of my gals were available on this 4th of July weekend and within twenty-four hours we were off to Maui, Hawaii. I was Babydol accompanying my alter ego Sasha's three girls.

As we sat there on the plane my Porn Star Jennifer turned and whispered something in my ear.

"Sash, I think I'm pregnant with Barry Bonds' baby!"

"No way! How did you meet him?" I asked.

"A friend brought me to a game and introduced me to him afterwards. He had his long, black limo waiting for him outside. After the game we went into the limo I fucked him right there in the back seat! He was so hot, Sash! Do all these baseball players have big, hot dicks?!"

"Wow girl! How long did you fuck him?" I asked.

"Well, if you ask me I could've stayed right there and fucked him forever!" Jennifer said.

"So, now what? What are you going to do?"

Jennifer began to tell me of her plans for baseball's bad boy Barry Bonds. She was late on her period and felt that Bonds was the father of her then unborn child. Her game plan was to have his baby, and get him to support her. She was asking me for advice. This would be one of several scandals I would find myself pulled into with this gal. I soon realized this once I received the call from Anthony Pellicano, also Michael Jackson's well known private investigator, some months after our return. He informed me that he had been tapping my telephone while representing Barry Bonds. He demanded to know what I knew about this Porn Star. This was at least six years prior to my conviction and high profile trial for running my escort empire. There was little I could tell him or admit to about anything as Sasha. Publicly, I was Babydol the recording artist with the famous billboard on Sunset Blvd.

An even bigger scandal I'd find myself in with this gal would be the O.J. Simpson case after confiding to me once again. I would come to learn from her own words that she was having an affair with O.J.'s best friend Al Cowlings, who drove his white bronco during their now infamous police chase. She had revealed that during a late night evening with Al over at O.J.'s house, O.J. had returned home screaming about his then living wife Nicole Brown. Apparently and according to her, O.J. had been hiding in the bushes spying on Nicole and was furious at what he had seen. Obviously, an admission that he was "stalking" his wife one week before her brutal murder was titanic! It wasn't long before Prosecuting Attorney Marcia Clarke got wind of it and sent twenty cops into her apartment to drag her down before the Grand Jury to testify. The now infamous double murder case would place O'.J. Simpson in a fight for his life, and my association with her during that time would soon have us both on prime time television and the 6 o' clock news.

We arrived in beautiful Maui, Hawaii and were met at the airport by a luxury stretch limo.

It had been an interesting flight and now we were taken to the hotel to get ready for dinner. So far, everything was going rather smoothly.

The evening began with dinner. The idea was that we would dine early, then meet outside to walk the red carpet and meet the press for the VIP opening before moving on to the private VIP party afterwards.

"Hi, I'm Babydol; and these are my friends Jennifer, Kim, and Debra" I said as we settled into our seats.

It seemed more appropriate to introduce them as my friends. My client Shep quickly slipped me the envelope with the money for the girls as he pulled over my chair before taking a seat of his own.

Seated to my right were Melanie Griffith, Sly, my three gals, Shep, and Arnold with wife Maria Schriver and their two body-guards. Now, most people would have felt that having Arnold there with his wife would mean that instantly nixed the possibilities of extra curricular activities with my girls. But, I knew better. There had been many times I'd seen men having sex with women while their wives were nearby sometimes even in the next room! Once Maria got up he winked at me with that "I'm trapped" look on his face. I wondered did he wink at me because he knew I'd brought the girls? Or was he just flirting? What I found most interesting however, was that every time Maria would leave the table to go to the ladies room the bodyguards were instructed to sit in the chair in her absence to insure that none of the gals would be given a chance to sit next to Arnold. Smart gal. I liked her style.   I never did condone married men cheating on their wives. But I had also learned early on in my career as a Hollywood Super Madam that it was not good for business to let my personal feelings and opinions get in the way. It really made no difference to my business deal here anyway for the girls were getting paid either way whether the guys went with them or not. As long as the decision not to indulge was a result of the guys and not the gals. The business end of things had been taken care of. I had already collected the money up front from Shep when he had quickly snuck me the envelope with the money in it earlier.

Whew! This really was a close one I thought. Somehow he never put it together that Babydol and Sasha were one and the same. And quite frankly how could he have? I had some practice doing this sort of thing many, many times before for years posing as my secretary Sherry on the phone with my girls. A necessary plan I had formulated to use for screening them before actually meeting them as Sasha. I had been doing this for a plethora of reasons including the demands of needing a secretary I felt I could trust but never find.

Dinner went well and it seemed everyone had enjoyed the simple menu the restaurant had to offer. But really, we were all looking forward to the private VIP party.

"Well, guess we better walk the red carpet and head towards the VIP party, huh?" Shep said.

Being Alice Cooper's manager had served him well and now he was a partner in a famous restaurant, too.

After dinner everyone walked the red carpet to the opening of yet another Planet Hollywood restaurant. I made my VIP entrance in a hot Versace jumpsuit. I had walked many red carpet events as Babydol and they were always lots of fun. We moved on to the VIP party upstairs where I noticed even more celebrities like Mike Myers, NBA player Robert Horry, and my gal pal, Rhonda Shear. She only knew me as Babydol and like everyone else in entertainment had no idea about my "double life" as Sasha. They wouldn't find that out until many years later when my arrest would make headlines on the news all over the world. I had been appearing as a celebrity guest on Rhonda's comedy show for the USA network "Up All Night" for two years so we were great friends and I enjoyed running into her. She would be quite shocked when the news broke of my arrest.

I was also keeping a watchful eye on my gals.

"Rhonda, sweetheart! What are you doing here? I didn't know you were coming!"

"I'm doing the red carpet thing. It's such fun!" she teased.

My eyes began to scan across the room as I realized I needed to stay on top of things with my girls. Sly had apparently liked my model and was sitting engrossed in conversation with her. I'd get the full report on that in the morning. My Porn Star had now completely run off with Robert Horry. The same gal who thought she was pregnant with Barry Bond's child. I noticed that Arnold was still sitting with his wife Maria remaining under her watchful eye for most of the evening. The rest of us all partied deep into the night.

The next morning we slept late and met outside by the pool at 4pm. We ordered Mai Tais. Today was our day to sit back and relax. We all got paid, had fun, and were now ready to dish Hollywood style. My model was nowhere to be found so

I knew she was still with Sly, which meant that my client Shep would be happy as he wanted to make a good impression. I had helped to close many a Hollywood movie deal this way by supplying the gals to investors, producers, or perhaps a famous movie star someone might be trying to lure into doing their film. I noticed my Porn Star Jennifer was still MIA too, so this meant she was still spending time with NBA player Robert Horry. If I know her she was probably fucking his brains out! That left my remaining gal the Playboy Playmate and myself to chat. She was a really pretty blonde Dutch gal 5' 8", about 22 yrs. So, I was rather surprised to see that she had not hooked up with anyone. The girls were only obligated to Sly & Arnold and since Arnold's wife Maria had never left his side that left only Sly who I knew was with my other model. But often it seemed the prettiest gals went home alone...

"That was fun last night, huh?" I began.

I took a decorative lounge chair in the sun seated next to her. Hawaii was so beautiful! Something about Maui always reminded me of the Garden of Eden.

"Oh, yeah!" she replied. "I got to talk to Mike Myers and met tons of people" she said.

"Cool. Hey, are you having any hot affairs with any celebrities back home right now?" I inquired.

I wanted to take full advantage of this moment.

"Sash, I can't say because he's 'cause still married."

I was alone with my girls and back to being Madam Sasha now.

"You know you're going to tell me everything so just stop" I said.

With all the many, many, girls vying for work and the enormous monies to be made with my service all the gals wanted me to like them and be considered first. So, I knew she'd break and tell.

"But you have to swear not to tell anyone" she begged.

"Alright, I swear."

I was dying to know who it was and whether he was a client of mine.

"It's Kevin Costner!" she confirmed.

"Oooh, he is sooo cute! Is he hot in bed?" I asked.

I was always eager for all the sexual details of any given experience.

"Yup, he sure is. He says he's going to be leaving his wife but I'm not holding my breath for that one! You know how married guys are. They always say that" she said.

"No doubt. What's his favorite thing to do in bed? Does he have a big dick?" I asked.

With a genuine appreciation for big dicks I was always eager to know who had one.

"His favorite thing is he loves eating pussy. And he's sooo good at it he can eat me for hours! Makes me cum over and over" she said.

I was getting hot again. Sex talk always got me wet.

"Yummy... that sounds so good!" I commented.

And with that my Porn Star Jennifer surfaced and walked over to join us. She was quite well known in adult films and I noticed lots of guys always recognized her.

"Well! How was your night?!" I began.

"Great!" I need a drink! Robert Horry fucked me all night with that big cock! He's flying me to meet him in Houston next week!" she stated proudly.

"Really? Isn't he married?" I asked.

Knowing of course, that probably didn't make a difference.

"Yup. It doesn't matter to me. I'm probably pregnant with Barry Bonds' baby anyway. I might as well get my fun in while I can. We exchanged phone numbers and he said he's getting me a ticket to fly out to see him there."

"Wow, girl, you must've done something right!" I laughed.

"You bet! I fucked him good and let him give it to me up my ass. That's my favorite you know" she added.

The truth was as Sasha, I was well aware of the fact that in her movies anal sex was her specialty along with gang bangs. I had booked her many times.

"Yes, darling. I'm well aware of that fact" I stated.

Anal sex was a particular specialty in the sex arena that clients paid quite a bit more for as most gals wouldn't do it.

"Here's to big cocks!" she said.

We all laughed and clicked our glasses.

"Great gig, Sash. Thanks. I guess our friend is still with Sly. Maybe he took her shopping" she continued.

"Hope so. We'll find out tomorrow on the flight home" I teased.

The rest of the afternoon we relaxed in the sun.

The following morning we were picked up by limo to go to the airport. Seated next to me was my model, the one who had been with Sly. I was eager to hear about her evening too.

"So, how did your evening go?" I began.

As usual, I wanted to hear all the juicy details. She was a real pretty gal, slim, and tall so I figured he liked her as that was his type.

"Aaaahhh. He was hot! A bit shorter than in the movies though...But what a body! I hope he sees me again when we get back" she said.

I knew that it was doubtful as Hollywood stars were not known for their monogamy especially with a movie star like Sly Stallone who had his choice of anyone he wanted. But, I wasn't cruel enough to hurt her feelings and tell her that. She wanted to believe it was love.

"What was his favorite position?" I asked.

"He liked me on top riding him. He is such a great kisser. And his muscles looked sooo fine!" she noted.

"I bet! How many times did he fuck you? Did he have a big dick?"

There I went with the big dick question again.

"Actually, his dick size was fine. He worked it real well and I'm in love with his hot bod!"

"Did he eat your pussy, too?" I inquired.

"Mmmm, a little. But mostly he liked to fuck and he loved me wrapping my long legs all over him."

"Sounds hot!" I commented.

The rest of the flight home was quiet as we were all lost in our thoughts...

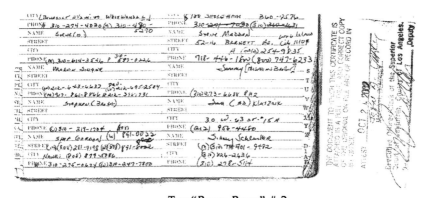

THE "BLACK BOOK" # 2
SHEP GORDON INSERT
OFFICIAL COURT SEAL OF AUTHENTICITY

Chapter 8: Bruce Willis

It was always terribly interesting the way people came to me as much of the time they did so in many different ways. Bruce Willis would prove to be no exception. I first got the call from my girl Lucia, in New York. It was a beautiful summer day in June. A stunning Brazilian gal with long beautiful brown hair, Lucia would be the one to send Bruce Willis to me that afternoon.

There was a sense of urgency in her voice as I listened to her page.

"Sash, it's Lucia. I really need to talk to you right away."

That was all her message said. I returned her call immediately as I always did with the girls.

"Hi, Lucia. It's Sash. What's up, sweetie?" I asked curiously.

"Sash, you'll never believe who I met! And he's going to phone you because he wants five girls for tonight in New York and I only have one girlfriend!" she stated in a panic.

"Who?" I asked curiously.

"Bruce Willis!" Lucia exclaimed.

I was accustomed to speaking with celebrities about sex but Lucia wasn't so it was no surprise that she was extremely excited.

"Aahhh, nice" I answered calmly.

"Five girls, huh? I've got lots of beauties in New York. Have him phone me immediately. I'll split my cut with you on your girlfriend" I offered.

I had sixteen offices in the United States and Europe so it was common for others to phone since I had the largest volume of girls. This was also a popular practice I shared with other madams. Anyone who sent the girl would receive half of my cut on the first job. Lucia was doing this by bringing to me her girlfriend and likely, her girlfriend would continue working with me afterwards.

"Okay. Right away. I have no idea what type he likes but he definitely wants five girls at once!" she said.

"Does he plan on having someone else join him or will he be alone?" I inquired.

After all, one never could tell as it could be a guy or a girl Bruce was bringing to join in. I'd learned early on never to assume anything. Perhaps he wanted to bring a new gal pal for an orgy. I'd booked scenarios like that before. I began to create a new file with his name on it.

"Not sure but he did mention some guy friend that produces all those Steven Segal movies. You talk to him" Lucia said.

I realized immediately that she was referring to producer Jules Nasso. He was the producer for most of those Steven Segal movies. But she didn't know that.

"I'll handle it and get back to you with all the specifics" I said.

"Okay, Sash. Thanks. Bye" Lucia ended as we hung up the phone.

Sure enough within a half hours time I received the call from Bruce. It seemed he wanted five hot girls for he and Jules Nasso.

."Hi, Bruce. It's nice to speak to you. Lucia mentioned you'd be calling. Sounds like quite a party" I teased him.

"Yeah, we hope so. Can you do it?" Bruce asked.

"Of course. I have many gorgeous gals like Lucia with my New York office. Look at my web site and see if there's anyone in particular you might like" I suggested.

"I have no time for that, Sasha. Here's the deal. Just pick five hot, young girls and make sure they can do each other because we really want a show! Figure on about two hours, max. We really don't have that much time to spend but we want them really hot and young!" Bruce said.

"I understand. How young?" I asked.

"Early twenties" Bruce answered.

I was relieved; it was my policy never to deal with any under-age girls, only girls of legal age 18 and over.

"Will you all be having sex together in one room?" I inquired.

This was essential in establishing the price. It was more expensive to have them all in one room, like an orgy.

"Oh, yeah. We want to party!" he laughed.

"Okay, then. Let's just make it a flat $3000 per girl for all five girls, total $15,000" I said.

I knew that would cover whatever might transpire although it was unlikely the guys would actually have that much sex with either girl with five to choose from. More like a sampling. But of course, they wouldn't realize that yet.

"Wow! That's pricey! $15,000 for pussy for one night?!" he exclaimed.

"Well, Bruce. You get what you pay for... there's always the Yellow Pages. Normally, for an orgy like this it would be $3000 per hour and I'm offering that to you as a total for your two hour requested time. So, I'm really giving you a deal. If you're not happy with the way they look when you open the door, you can send whichever one away and I'll send someone else."

I knew this would never happen since the gals I dealt with were some of the most beautiful Playmates and models in the world. Besides, it was more likely they'd be anxious to get started right away once they saw how pretty the girls were. My New York office was one of my biggest offices and I had no shortage of available gorgeous girls there that would want to make money and party with Bruce Willis.

At the time of my arrest and during my trial, the prosecution made sure to document the fact I had well over 300 girls, along with my sixteen offices in the United States and Europe which they made sure to use as evidence against me.

"Okay, Sash. You win... fifteen thousand bucks. I'll phone back in a half hour with the hotel info" Bruce said.

"Okay. Please have everything ready in one envelope and give it to Lucia. She'll pay the girls" I suggested.

"No problem. Speak with you then."

Bruce did indeed phone back as promised with the hotel info. I phoned Lucia and I clued her in on the plan, placing her in charge of handling the money as she had done for me many times before. Her end on this job would be $1800. Plus, half of my $1200 cut on her friend would leave her with $2400 for two hours. My cut was 40% although most madams took 50%. The other three girls I booked were my girls in NY. Lucia would be holding $5400 for me; her cut of $1200, plus her friend's $600, and the $1200 each from the remaining three girls.

But it wasn't the first time as she had handled money in larger amounts for me before so I knew I could trust her.

I began to make the necessary calls to my girls in NY, sure they would be thrilled. Lucia would be happy, Bruce and Jules would have a blast, and I was pleased.

A real win, win situation. That's how it is and that's sex in Hollywood.

"Sasha, do I know the other three girls you're sending?" Lucia asked when I phoned her back.

"No, Love. I don't think I've booked you with them before. There's Donna; she's a blonde about 5'6". And Debbie; who's also blonde but a bit taller. Both gals are on the busty side. The other is Danielle; a real pretty French gal. She's actor Joe Pesci's girlfriend but they're fighting right now so don't mention anything to her about him."

"Oh, I think I saw her in the tabloids! She's beautiful!" Lucia commented.

"Yes, she is... blonde with shoulder length hair, about a 34B. Not too busty. She's not sure if she wants to stay with Joe and have his baby because she's pregnant or leave him. She complains that he doesn't help her much with any money" I confided.

"That's odd. Oh, well. Anyway, did Bruce discuss the specifics with you about the party?" she asked.

"Yes. He's bringing his producer friend and you're all going to have an orgy together. You'll be paid $3000 each. I'm splitting my $1200 cut with you because you're bringing your girlfriend. Which means you'll clear $2400, and hold $5400 for me" I instructed.

"Sounds good, Sash. Will we be meeting them at their hotel? They can all come to my place if they like. I've got plenty of room and a huge bed" Lucia offered.

"I hadn't thought of that but I'll phone him back right now and see."

I phoned Bruce back and it seemed he liked the idea of having this kind of party in a more private place then the hotel suite he was staying in.

"Lucia, it looks like he'd prefer to come to you. What's your address? I'll give it to the other gals as well."

"Okay. I'm at 222 E. 58th St., Apt 2C. Shall I phone you when everyone gets here to check in?" she asked.

''No, that's okay. Just call if you need me, or if one of the girls does a no show."

Unlikely that would happen on a great gig like this and a chance to meet Bruce Willis in the nude.

"Okay, then. Speak with you tomorrow" she finished.

The following morning I waited for Lucia's call. I was anxious to hear every juicy detail of her hot evening with Bruce and Jules and I loved hearing about sex. It was late in the afternoon when I received it.

"Hi, Lucia. It's Sash. So, do tell." I teased.

"Wow! Well, he certainly is the stud, Sash! First, the two gals you sent Donna and Debbie stripped for all of us and put on a really hot sex show. Were they dancers? Because they sure looked like they'd done this before! We watched while they first danced real sexy. Then, they started workin' it and began to eat each other's pussy. At that point we all took our clothes off and everybody really got into it. That's when Bruce had me take off my g-string panties and sit on his face while he ate my pussy and my ass. He was sooo hot! He really could work his tongue on my clit and my asshole! My girlfriend sat on his dick and rode him for like a half hour. She and I switched and I fucked him too. He has a hot, big dick Sash!" she said.

"Well, I figured that. He looks like he does." I answered.

"We didn't really do much with the other guy. He 'kinda fell for one of the gals and she got on him and started fucking him and wouldn't let go! Then my girlfriend and I went to work on Bruce with the double blowjob. Looks like he was having most of the fun! He really wanted to shoot his cum all over her face but she wouldn't let him. She made him cum on her tits. Real hot though! The time flew by!" she said.

I was glad to see Bruce got his money's worth.

"I've got your money, Sash. Should I FedEx today?" Lucia inquired.

"Sounds like a great evening! How long did you stay?" I asked.

"It seemed like longer but I think it was less than two hours. I have your $5400 cut for you" she said.

"Actually sweetie, I'm coming in to NY next week to handle some business. I'll be there in a few days. Why don't you just give it to me then. I'll take you to lunch someplace like the '21 Club or something" I suggested.

Normally, I always insisted the girls forward me whatever balances were due to avoid any snafus with the responsibilities of money. But, I knew Lucia was pretty reliable and since I was on my way there in 72 hours, lunch sounded like a fun thing to do.

"We can chat more about things then" I suggested.

You never could be sure though, when it came to girls holding onto money as anything could happen. That was also a lot of money to send in the mail. She had been responsible for much more for me in the past so I opted to wait until we met. We would catch up on more of those juicy sex details I loved hearing about later.

"Sounds good. I'll hold onto it and you can call me and let me know when and where you want to meet when you get in. Oh, and thanks, Sash, for handling all this. It was really cool" Lucia finished.

"Great. I'll phone tomorrow from the plane" I finished as we said our goodbyes for now...

BRUCE WILLIS
212-759-3000

BRUNO FRNDEZ
917 971 9847

BRUNO(GUESS)
213 235 3300

THE DOCUMENT TO WHICH THIS CERTIFICATE IS
ATTACHED IS A FULL, TRUE, AND CORRECT COPY
OF THE ORIGINAL ON FILE AND OF RECORD IN
MY OFFICE. *Pages: 9 -10 -13 -31 -41 -53 -55 -57 -59*

ATTEST _____ OCT 2 4 2002

JAMES A. DEMPSEY

Executive Officer/Clerk of the Superior
Court of California, County of Los Angeles.
By _____ ,Deputy

9

PRINTOUT FROM "WIZARD" #3
BRUCE WILLIS
OFFICIAL STAMPED COURT SEAL OF AUTHENTICITY

Chapter 9: Maurice Marciano of Guess

Maurice Marciano was the owner of the Guess Empire. He was a lovely European client along with some of his staff. One sunny afternoon I received a call from him requesting three gorgeous girls for himself and two others. His associate, Bruno got on the phone.

Maurice had his assistant Bruno phone to ask that the girls meet them first for lunch at a very chic French restaurant in town. I had a beautiful blonde named Beth and two lovely brunettes all ages 24-28 in mind. I knew them to be lovely clients that would likely begin with a lavish lunch. The girls would be treated like royalty before moving on to a suite at the Beverly Hills Hotel for some intimate playtime.

"Hello, Bruno. How are you and Maurice doing? The ads for Guess seem to be getting more beautiful every year!" I began.

"Oh, Sasha. We are doing fabulous. Three of us would like three of your beautiful girls to meet us for lunch at Café Moustache on Melrose around 1pm today. Then, we have some suites at the Beverly Hills Hotel" Bruno answered.

"Sounds like a lovely day. Will Maurice be joining you as well?" I asked.

European clients were very particular about the type they preferred and most leaned towards the taller, smaller busted, model types as opposed to my busty California Gal look. I always had to make sure I had enough variety to offer them.

"Yes, it will be Maurice, myself and one other. You have the three available for us today?" he asked.

"Of course, you know I do! Don't I always?" I teased.

"Yes, Sasha. You always do" he confirmed.

"So, Bruno, tell me, Darling. Are you all planning on a party in one suite or will you be pairing off to separate suites?" I inquired.

Knowing these kind of specifics were essential in establishing my prices. A party in one suite might mean that each girl would take more than one man, switching sexual partners and that would make the party more expensive.

"I believe we intend to pair off into separate suites" Bruno said.

"Alright, then. Shall we say lunch plus $1000 per girl for an hour party after? That would make it $3000 total for your party. Unless you think you'll be spending more private time than usual."

Maurice and his staff were good and frequent clients but generally preferred a long lunch followed by an hour with the girls.

"That sounds fine, Sasha. We will see them there then at 3pm."

"No problem, Bruno. Have fun" I said.

I hung up to phone the girls. I went to my file marked "Girls". My Yorkie, Killer, was anxious to go outside and play with the other 32 larger sized dogs. The Yorkies, Killer and Cupcake, along with my white Maltese Caesar, were the little ones who got to live inside the house with me. I opened the large glass door which led outside to his freedom.

Mmmmm, I thought. Let's see here. After flipping through the file I decided on which three girls to send for the afternoon lunch. I reached over to my pink cell phone used for the girls and began to dial Bethanee's number. The black cell phone I used was for my male clients and lay lined up next to the pink one. There were five phones in all; one for gals, one for guys, one for International calls, one for when I was out on the water, and my house land line phone reserved for home emergencies only.

I never used my actual home line phone for doing business. It was too risky.

"Bethanee, honey, it's Sasha. Are you free for a lunch date this afternoon? I began.

"Hi, Sash. Yes, I sure am" she answered.

"Good. It's at Café Moustache on Melrose. You'll see two of my other girls there. You'll all start with lunch and then move on to private suites at the Beverly Hills Hotel. It'll be one guy per girl for an hour for $1000" I said.

"That's cool. I'll be there. Will they be leaving their names for us?" Bethanee asked.

"Yes, just have them show you to the Marciano table."

"What? Is that Marciano as in Guess?" she exclaimed.

"Sure is, sweetie."

"Wow! That's cool! I have always wanted to meet those guys! Okay, then. I'll jump in the shower" she said excited.

"Great. Call me and check in when you get there. Bye" I finished.

I realized I still had to phone the two other girls. I did and fortunately they were both available to be there by 3pm.

When it came to the world of escorts one had to learn how to get clothes and make up on quickly and run out the door while remaining cool, calm, and collected. One of my Agency Rules was 'never be late' and 'always show up to a call relaxed. No matter what set of circumstances had just transpired moments before. Walking in calmly with a smile was much more attractive then showing up out of breath babbling on about your bad day. So far, it seemed the afternoon was off to a good start.

It was 4 o'clock as I waited for the phone call from the girls to check in. Suddenly, I received a page from one of the girls asking me to phone her over at the room which I did immediately. She sounded a bit alarmed. The girls always knew if anything at all needed to be worked out or any of the details of the job were to vary from the specifics I outlined earlier, they were to phone me and I would take care of things. I discouraged the girls from ever handling any difficulties themselves that might arise especially when it came to money. I preferred to be the 'bad guy.' This way we could usually still salvage the deal in case things hadn't started off quite right.

"Sash" she began "They want us all to party in the same suite. I'm okay with it and so are the other girls but shouldn't we be getting a bit more money for this kind of request?"

Bethanee was smart and familiar with the agency rules.

"Yes, sweetie. Put Bruno on the phone, please."

Bruno was the one who not only organized the scenarios but handled all the details as well.

"Bruno, Hi, it's Sasha. Listen, are you having a good time?" I asked.

"Oh, yes, Sasha. Thank you. The girls are wonderful" he said.

"Great" I continued. "Beth says you're planning a party with all of you in the same suite. That's fine, Darling, but we'll have to change the price we agreed on."

I knew full well that it would be highly unlikely they would want to stop now.

"Oh, sooo sorry, Sasha. How much more will they need?" he asked.

"Well, we agreed on lunch plus an hour in the room for $1000 per girl so now you'll need to give each girl $500 apiece more if you all want to watch each other in the same room. Which means a total of $4500 instead of $3000. And it's still one guy per girl or I'll have to double each fee. But you can all watch each other and the girls can play with each other too."

"No problem, Sasha. One guy to one girl. I'll take care of things immediately and include the extra $500 per girl" he assured me.

"Thanks, Honey. Now please put Bethanee back on the phone."

When he did I said

"Hi, Sweetie. Everything's been worked out so you'll each get $1500 instead if $1000. It's still one guy per girl but you girls can tease them a bit with a girlie show. Be sure not to take more than one guy" I warned.

Bethanee's quick thinking meant an extra $300 for each of the girls and an additional $200 per girl for me, which equaled an added $600.

"Great. Got it. I'll tell the others" she answered. "Thanks, Sash. Talk to you later."

Later that evening, Bethanee and I met at the usual place to settle up

"Sash, I'm sooo grateful for this gig. You know, I've got a little ten month old baby at home I'm raising myself. With all the scandal about poor child care I'm scared to death to leave anyone with him! So, getting a job is out of the question. My mom watches him from time to time, but having you there enables me to make my entire rent in one or two nights! I just wanted you to know that" she said.

"Thank you, sweetie. I'm glad I could be there. Raising a child as a single parent must be difficult."

"Yeah, it is. But at least this way, I can be with my baby".

"I understand. Anytime" I finished.

MAURIC(GUESS
213 765 3535

MECHANIC
818 507 5016

MEGAN(BAROCA
310 301 1628

MEISSA(PAGER
310 586 5228

MEL
201 370 5350

MEL(ARTHUR)
619 318 9388

THE "WIZARD" #3 PRINTOUT
BRUNO/ GEORGE MARCIANO OF GUESS
OFFICIAL COURT SEAL OF AUTHENTICITY

BRUCE WILLIS
212-759-3000

BRUNO FRNDEZ
917 971 9847

BRUNO(GUESS)
213 235 3300

THE DOCUMENT TO WHICH THIS CERTIFICATE IS
ATTACHED IS A FULL, TRUE, AND CORRECT COPY
OF THE ORIGINAL ON FILE AND OF RECORD IN
MY OFFICE.

ATTEST _____ OCT 2 4 2002

JAMES A. CLARKE

Executive Officer/Clerk of the Superior
Court of California, County of Los Angeles.
By _____ ,Deputy

9

Chapter 10: Mark Wahlberg & Bo Dietl Party

Everyone knew who "Marky Mark" was especially after all those hot Calvin Klein billboards of him in his underwear. But at first I did not know about Bo Dietl until he phoned.

It was somewhere in the mid 90's perhaps 1996 or 1997. They were staying at the Peninsula Hotel in Beverly Hills and Bo was in town because they were preparing to do the movie on his life story and considering Mark Wahlberg for the part before ultimately giving it to actor Steven Baldwin. After some research on Bo, I found out who he was and learned that he had been a decorative cop in NY for years before turning in his entire precinct for being dirty cops... real fascinating stuff that Hollywood movies are made of.

I don't recall who it was that referred him to me but with my strict policies it had to be someone whom I knew well. Quite frankly, as I had most of the concierges and valets from all the major upscale hotels on my payroll they always notified me when a wealthy or famous client was in town looking for company. I rewarded them with a "kickback" which was a cut of what I made. So, it would likely just have been a matter of time before these two found me anyway.

"Hi, Bo. It's Sasha. What can I do for you?" I began.

"Sasha, Sasha, Sasha! Am I glad to talk to you!" he said. "I'm in town here at this beautiful hotel with Mark Wahlberg and we're looking to party tonight."

"No problem, Bo. Any particular type you have in mind?" I asked.

"A couple of hot, young, busty blondes would be nice!"

"Only a couple?" I teased. "Well, we have plenty of that. Bo, are you two in separate rooms or will you all be partying together in one suite?"

"We've got a few rooms but I have no idea how the evening will turn out, Sasha. Does it matter?" he asked.

"Yes, it does affect the price. It's more expensive if you'd like the girls to switch off with you, or all party together. But there is no problem in providing you with whatever you desire" I confirmed.

"Mmmmm, now you've got me thinking. How much?" he asked.

Men always got right to the point with that one.

"Well, let me ask you a few things first. Is there anything in particular you're into that I should know? Anal, Dominance, role play, girl on girl?"

It was important to first establish the sexual specifics to determine which girls to send.

"Wow! Sounds like we can get just about anything we want, huh?" he sounded surprised.

"You sure can. How long are you figuring to keep the girls?" I asked.

"Just a few hours. We've still got some late night business to take care of. Nothing too unusual. Some straight ahead fucking or maybe a great blow job" he answered.

"Ok, then if it's just two girls in two separate rooms for say 2 hours, it's $2000 each. If you want the girls to switch off with you; meaning that you'll each have both girls, than it's $3000 each for the two hours" I said.

"Got it. Seems like I should be in your business, huh, Sash! We'll do the two hot busty blondes, in two separate rooms for the $2000 ea. We'd love to party more but we really can't stay too long tonight. Maybe next time" he finished.

"Alright. Sounds great. You know its cash only."

"Yes, Sash. I know the drill."

"What are the room numbers?" I said almost forgetting to ask.

Bo gave me their room numbers and I began flipping through my file marked 'Girls. Apparently, he had dabbled in this before. Actually, other escort services had no problem accepting other forms of payment besides cash. But as that was not my policy I always had to specify things.

"Hey, thanks" he said.

"Okay, have fun" I answered.

I immediately found two beautiful 22 yr old busty, blondes I was sure they'd love and since it didn't require a bi-sexual scene it was an easy order to fill.

"Kelly, girl. It's Sasha. I hope you're up for a party tonight!" I started.

"Sash! Hi. What's up? Yeah, I'm around, anything good?" she began.

"Oh, yes! How does Mark Wahlberg sound to you?" I teased.

"Ooooh, I love him! Really?" she asked.

Kelly was about 5 10", a natural 38c, Pam Anderson type with a beautiful face. She'd had a hot affair with a high profile athlete and guys really liked her.

"You bet. They're staying at the Peninsula Hotel in Beverly Hills. They want you and another girl there tonight at 8pm. You'll both be in separate rooms, though".

"Okay. That's fine. Who's the other girl you're sending?" she asked.

"Did you meet a pretty blonde with me named Casey? She's a real sweetheart."

"I think so. What's the room info and how much?" she asked.

A real pro, Kelly could get right to the point.

"You'll get $2000 each, for two hours. They're in rooms 510 and 511. Make sure you phone me in the event they want an orgy party because that will cost them more" I confirmed.

"You got it! Thanks, Sash. I'll check in later" she finished.

I noticed it was already 5pm. Fortunately, Casey had been home when I gave her the information as well.

I waited for the girls to phone later that evening. It was around 1am when they did. Kelly was the first to phone.

"Hey, Sash. It's Kelly. The evening went really well. I was with Bo and I saw your other girl on the way in to Mark's room. Lucky gal. I bet he was a hot fuck!" she laughed.

"No doubt. I'll let you know since I'm still waiting for her to phone. What did Bo want?"

It was time to get the skinny on the sexual specifics.

"Oh, he was real easy. I sucked his cock and then fucked him but really I wasn't there but for an hour, tops" she said.

"Really? He had a good time though, didn't he?"

I did not encourage the girls to ever rush with clients even though time was money. A client could easily sense that so the girls had to play it smart.

"Oh, he was definitely happy, Sash. I made him cum twice" she said.

"Sounds like an easy one. Call me tomorrow and we'll figure out where to meet" I finished.

I was more interested in the sexual details of Mark Wahlberg. He always seemed like a hot stud that probably had a big dick and was a great fuck. Since my other girl was obviously still occupied with him I assumed I was right.

Her page came in several hours later.

"Sash, I'm in love!" she began.

"Now, now. You know better than that" I warned.

"I know. But he's the hottest guy I've ever been with! He fucked me on my side with his arms wrapped around me.

Pumping his big dick from behind slowly, slowly for a long time too. Then he plowed me faster and faster when he was about to cum! He shot the biggest load all over my ass! I stayed way longer than I should without asking for more money so I hope you're not mad."

"Sweetie, you know how this game works. Mark Wahlberg is a gorgeous famous movie star and for all we know he could be engaged! You know better than to get emotionally involved with a client! Especially someone like him! He's likely got a thousand girls in love with him! So what did you get for the extra time? Just the $2000?" I asked.

"Yeah. No tip either. But he was a real romantic fuck! I should've paid him! Please tell me you're not mad" she pleaded.

"No, I'm not mad. But try to remember what you're dealing with here and keep your eye on the ball" I suggested.

Of course I totally understood her attraction for a hot stud like Mark. But often, I had to remind the girls and give them a reality check from time to time...

THE "BLACK BOOK" # 2
BO DIETL
OFFICIAL COURT SEAL OF AUTHENTICITY

Chapter 11: Supermodel Naomi Campbell's Father Ernesto

The Arab Royals were a select group often with unusual life-style habits. They had a preference for extremely young girls. I had a policy to deal only with girls of legal age so often, I would send them gals in their early twenties that perhaps looked eighteen or younger. I was well aware that if they had their way they would have requested ages thirteen through sixteen.

I didn't care much for them as clients and only dealt with a chosen few. It seemed that even with all their enormous wealth they enjoyed attempting to get away with refusing to pay for services rendered at all. This prompted me early in my career to develop my "pay up front" approach, which they frowned upon, but ultimately acquiesced to. They had an insatiable appetite for women often only seeing a gal once and then immediately ready for someone new. I was one of the few Madams with that kind of volume, which explained why they put up with it.

The girls complained that the Middle Eastern men didn't bathe enough and were extremely hairy, often refusing attention to their hygiene. Their unusual lifestyle habits also included sleeping most of the day while remaining up all night. A girl really had to be a night owl if she wanted to make money with the Arabs. Their main meal was served late at 9pm and was quite heavy to have at that hour. It was not uncommon to see them dine on lamb, red meat, rice, and some of their more exotic choices all of which seemed to be an unhealthy choice for late night dining. Fortunately, they always had an open kitchen with a chef or the girls might not have eaten at all during their long stays with them.

Rarely did they dress in anything other than their long white nightgowns called Thobes. Some of the younger more sophisticated Royals did show up in pants and a shirt every now and then but the older gentlemen definitely remained in their Thobes.

In my dealings with thousands of men I found that Middle Eastern men had a sexual preference for anal sex. I was able to accommodate this but only with a few as most of the girls did not care much for it. The men also enjoyed having a finger placed up their own ass, along with asking the girls to wear a strap on dildo to penetrate them with. The girls that did participate in their sexual exploits made quite a bit more money than the other's. If a Royal Prince enjoyed the company of a young girl who could provide for his kinky needs, she would be rewarded with huge lavish shopping sprees on Rodeo Dr. where money was no object sometimes returning with over $100,000 in couture clothes and expensive diamond jewelry.

The Princes and Royals rarely did anything for themselves. It seemed they all had a "front man." He was the one who was in charge of their diet, shopped for them, chose their women, and probably wiped their ass when they went to the bathroom as well. One of these front men was Supermodel Naomi Campbell's father Ernesto, a short Arab man, quite educated and sophisticated who did virtually everything for my client, his employer Prince Sataam.

The Royal Prince Saatam owned many homes and traveled all over the world but their summers were spent in Los Angeles, California. By late April I would receive the call from Ernesto.

"Sasha, we are coming. Have the girls ready" is all he would say.

Although I had their private phone numbers from Paris to Riad, Saudi Arabia there was really no need for calls as they were here like clockwork every May. I was grateful for the business.

They could go through an enormous amount of girls so I did need to be prepared. On the average, they usually spent upwards of $1,000,000 during that time with me.

Prince Sataam was one of the nicer gentleman whose palatial estate took up an entire street in Bel Air known as St. Pierre. He actually owned two gorgeous Tudor style mansions one right next to the other. The grounds were immaculately kept with the most spectacular gardens and selections of flowers, which were well hidden behind huge iron gates. On each estate rested a separate maids quarters the size of an ordinary house, along with a smaller home made up of retired police officers and security guards hired to keep a watchful eye on the compound. The inside of these homes were elegantly furnished in an antique but simple style with the most of the furniture custom designed in silk Moray. As a fan of antique furniture I had some of my own furniture upholstered like that in the past so I was familiar with the beauty of a material like silk Moray.

Often, I would spend time with Ernesto in their home as I waited to retrieve my suitcase full of cash. Ernesto was one of the only clients privy to meeting me as the madam, Sasha. But it had become necessary with the large amounts of money that were being passed. I had insisted on a rather particular arrangement with the Prince as I was concerned about the girls being responsible for these enormous amounts of cash. It was not uncommon for a gal to make as much as $100,000 for spending time with the Prince.

Sometimes, the girls would phone me in the middle of the night.

"Sash, the Prince took some pills and he's been asleep for the last three days! What should I do?" she asked.

"Read a book or something! Don't wake him up! Honey, there are worse ways to make $25,000 a week! "I said. Geez!

I decided it would be best if Ernesto paid the girls their end and held my cut for me, hence my need to make a rare appearance to retrieve my suitcase full of cash which they were always good for year after year, after year. Ernesto was kind and well mannered and we always had a fun time together laughing and carrying on.

We became good friends and after a while he confided in me that he was Supermodel Naomi Campbell's father. I would be sitting there when a call from Naomi would come in from Paris. I sat and watched while they spoke French, which fortunately, I spoke as well although not nearly as well as he. Sometimes, Ernesto would hang up the phone and complain.

"That was Naomi calling me because she ran out of money again!" he would say.

I found that rather hard to believe. Supermodel Naomi Campbell running out of money? But heard it myself sitting right there. Guess things were always different than they seemed.

One afternoon, we were having a drink and chatting when his cell phone rang. As he became engrossed with his call I noticed a basket on the coffee table with some CDs and cassette tapes in it. Somewhat bored while waiting for him I began to surf through the collection and noticed something fascinating. Amongst this pile was a CD with the name clearly marked Claudia Schiffer on it. A bit startled I picked it up for a closer look. It was written in black marker. This made me think. Was Naomi bringing girls here to meet the Prince? After all, Ernesto did complain that she needed more money. And if so, how much would a Supermodel command for such a visit? Many questions ran through my mind as I waited for him to finish up his call. When he did he returned his attentions to me.

"Ernesto" I began cautiously "Does Naomi ever visit here and bring any of her Supermodel friends?" I inquired.

I was careful not to offend one of my biggest clients, even though I was oozing with curiosity.

"Oh, yes. Claudia was just here recently and she's brought some others" he replied.

I began to wonder why a Supermodel like Naomi Campbell would bring her Supermodel friends here. One could understand perhaps once in a while to see her father and visit the spectacular grounds of Bel Air while enjoying a stay in Los Angeles. But Ernesto made it sound like it happened on a somewhat more frequent basis then once in awhile. I wasn't sure whether to continue this line of questioning for obvious reasons. Were the Supermodels being paid to be here? Was Naomi getting a cut? If so, were the Supermodels indulging in sex with the Prince as well or was it more like a paid celebrity appearance? As this conversation was most delicate I felt it best not to ask. Which is why I was most surprised with what Ernesto said next;

"Yes, the Supermodels get $100,000 a week here. Naomi just brought Linda Evangelista!" he blurted out.

Wow! I thought. My girls were getting $25,000 per week. I guess it paid to be a Supermodel in more ways than one. That's pretty interesting. However, as I was there to retrieve a suitcase with a large amount of cash I thought it best to let it go and did not pursue the conversation further. Nor did I feel Ernesto would have told me much more. Further questioning might alienate him and I certainly did not want that. I decided to leave well enough alone for now. My temptation for juicy sexual details was gnawing at me... However, my sense of self-restraint and fondness for making money was stronger.

I said my goodbyes for that day and left there with my suitcase full of cash.

THE "BLACK BOOK" # 2
SUPERMODEL NAOMI CAMPBELL'S FATHER ERNESTO
OFFICIAL COURT SEAL OF AUTHENTICITY

Chapter 12: Tommy La Sorda

It was a cloudy day in July when I received the call from my client Jim in Chicago. He was phoning to send a new client to me.

"Hi, Sash. It's Jim. Call me back. I've got someone real interesting to introduce you to" his message said.

I always returned calls from good clients immediately and Jim was a good client.

"Hi, Jim. How's the weather in Chicago today?"

"Alright I suppose. I'd rather be in Los Angeles with all your hot girls" he teased.

"Can't blame you there, Jim. What's up?" I asked.

"I've got a real winner of a client for you. He's a high profile older guy."

"Really?" I answered curiously. "Who is it?"

"It's Tommy La Sorda" Jim said.

"The baseball legend?" I asked.

"The very one. Shall I have him phone you? He'll mention my name, of course."

Jim was most familiar with my referral policy.

"Sure. Any idea what he's looking for?" I asked.

"No, but he'll tell you."

"Sounds great! Thanks, Jim. Will we be seeing you anytime soon?" I asked.

"Not likely, Sash. I'd love to but I'm stuck here on business."

"Okay, then. Speak with you next time. Oh, and Jim don't forget to send him to my web site so he can see the girls" I suggested.

"Got it, Sash. See 'ya."

About an hour or so later Tommy La Sorda did indeed call. I returned his page to the number he left me.

"Hi, Tommy. This is Sasha. I understand you're a friend of Jim's?" I began.

"Yeah, sure am. He said some real nice things about you" he said.

"Aawww, he's a sweetheart. Thank you. So, what can I do for you today?" I asked.

"I'm interested in spending some time with someone."

"Sounds fine. Have you had a chance to look at my California Dreamin' web site? Perhaps there's someone there that you like" I suggested.

"Actually, I have. There's a pretty blonde on there I'd like to meet. # 6" he said.

"She's a sweetie. Her name is Nanna. She's Swedish, about 5' 6", nice perky 34b, slim, and terrific company. Perhaps you can tell me what you're looking for? Anything in particular I should know?"

I had to ask the standard question.

"Actually, Sash, I'd like her to have some porn for me to watch while she sucks my cock. I'm into watching two gals together in a movie. Can she have that there?" he questioned it as if it were a real unusual request.

I started a file on Tommy and began to make the pertinent notes.

'Likes girl, girl porn while having his cock sucked.'

It was important to keep track of all the little particulars that each client desired.

"No problem with either request. Not only is she a real pretty gal but she's particularly good at oral sex so you've got the right gal. I'll make sure she's got the movies on hand. How much time are you looking to spend?" I inquired.

"I'm not sure…. maybe, an hour and a half. I don't have that much time. How much for that?" he asked.

"It's $1000 per hour. So, that would cost you $1500. You can visit with her at her place. She lives in the Hollywood area."

"That sounds fine, Sash. I'm looking to get together this week. I'm thinking Thursday late afternoon. I've got to get home to the wife for dinner" he said.

"Got it. Did Jim mention it's cash payment only?"

"No, he didn't. But that's fine."

"Alright, Tommy. Phone me back when you're sure of your plans and I'll arrange everything for you" I offered.

"Will do, Sasha. Talk to you then" Tommy said in that husky voice of his.

Tommy phoned back the following day with the information.

My next call was to Nanna, the lovely blonde Swedish gal that Tommy liked. She was darling and a real pro although great at concealing that fact. The secret of the gorgeous gal… never let on just how much you really know. Men like to believe in a girl's innocence. You could never tell looking at Nanna that she was one of the best little cock suckers in town. At least the guys thought so.

Nanna answered the phone when I called.

"Hi, Nanna. It's Sasha. How are you today?"

"I'm fine, Sash. I hope you're calling with a booking for me. I just got a huge cell phone bill!" she said.

The girls knew working with me was a lot like having a best friend at a bank. Whenever they needed money all they had to do was call. They could tell me how much they needed to make and I could help them get it. I was always there for them when they needed me in addition to being a travel agent, babysitter, therapist, etc.

"I've got a booking for you tonight with someone really famous" I continued.

"Really, who?" she asked.

"Baseball legend Tommy La Sorda". I said.

"Hey, that's cool. He's a bit older, no?" she asked in that slight Swedish accent she still had.

It sounded terribly cute.

"Yes, he is. I bet he'll be real easy, too. He wants a great blowjob while watching some good porn videos. Got any?" I asked.

"I'm sure I do."

"Okay, because he specified a girl, girl movie. If you don't have any let me know and I'll get one from one of the girls so you don't have to buy one" I offered.

With all the porn stars employed with my service there was no need to purchase an adult film unless one had a particular film star in mind that I didn't know. And I knew a great majority of them.

"The booking is for tomorrow afternoon at your place at 3 pm, for about an hour and a half, for $1500 dollars. You know the drill. Just please make sure the porn movie you've got has some real girl, girl action because that's what he's looking for. In fact, if you have more than one that would be great" I instructed.

Clients could be very specific about what they were looking for.

"No problem. I'll be ready" she said.

"Good. Call me afterwards."

"Okay, Sash. Thanks. Bye."

The rest of my day was rather hectic since I still had the Royal Prince in town. With their especially late hours and all the girls they went through, I never got enough sleep. Nanna had seen them already last year and done quite well with them. After staying three weeks she had made $75,000. Her cut of which was $45,000. They loved her type but almost never saw the same girls again. New girls and volume was everything with them.

The following day I awoke still exhausted from my late night before. It was Thursday morning, 6:30 am. I had been up all night with the Arabs as they had asked for more girls then usual. Added relatives were in town. I was accustomed to the early mornings to deal with my boys on Wall St in my NY office. That was where my real money was made. They were in the office by 10 am, EST time, and I was in Los Angeles on PST time, which meant they were three hours ahead. I had to be ready for them. Most of my NY Wall St clients had already made their first million before the age of 39! Many were married and already living with their wives in a big mansion in Long Island. They kept the wives busy out there, while running around with the other gals in the city during the week. Weekends kept the married ones at home but you could always count on them to book girls to play with during the week. It would be a busy night in NY until Friday when it would all come to a halt. Weekends my NY office was quiet. But by noon later today my pager would be off the hook with calls for tonight.

I knew I had a busy day ahead of me so I was ready with my gourmet cinnamon hazelnut coffee, and CNN or Fox news. Gourmet coffee was my drug of choice and I required my two cups every morning. I was a news information junkie and always began my mornings like this. I also remembered this was the day Nanna was going to see Tommy La Sorda and I was looking forward to hearing all about him afterwards.

At 5pm later that afternoon I heard from Nanna. I remembered how Tommy had specified the need to be home early to join his family for dinner.

"Hi, Nanna. How'd everything work out?" I began.

"He was super easy and a really nice guy. You were right on all counts, Sasha. First, he requested I pop in my girl, girl porn movie. I had several at home since we know it's a popular request with the guys. He just loved watching all that! I noticed though, that he wasn't the aggressive type" she said.

"Really? What makes you say that?" I asked.

"Well, here I had this real hot porn movie on. He enjoyed watching the girl, girl bisexual sex scenes the best. He started to take his dick out and jerk off. Then, when I saw he was good and hard I started to suck his cock. He really liked that! I used your "Swirly" Move and relaxed my throat muscles so I could take him deep in my throat. The great blowjob skills you taught me plus the porn really got him off!" she said.

I had often trained many of the gals in the art of oral sex. I affectionately deemed it "Sasha's crash course". It was critical to knowing how to handle men sexually as I always reminded them that

"the way to his heart is definitely through your blow job".

"Of course, Darling. It's a winning combination!" I joked as we laughed.

"He seemed like he wanted to see me again so I told him to phone you. I'd be into it if he wants to."

She was also familiar with my 'No phone number exchanges in my 'Agency Rules'.

"I got the $1500 so let me know when you want to meet to settle up" Nanna said.

This meant Nanna was holding my cut of $600. It paled in comparison to the much larger amounts she'd held for me in the past so I wasn't really in any hurry to rush out and meet her.

"Tomorrow afternoon okay? Say about 3pm at the usual place" I suggested.

"That's fine. See you there. Thanks, Sash."

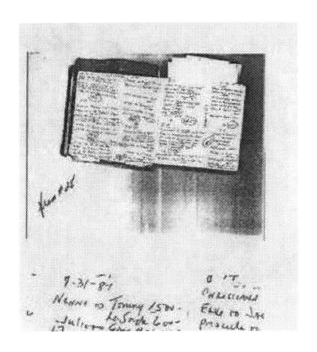

EXHIBIT 25: THE "BLACK BOOK" # 1
TOMMY LA SORDA
OFFICIAL COURT SEAL OF AUTHENTICITY

Chapter 13: Ben Barnes, House of Representatives, Lt. Governor of Texas

B en Barnes was a high profile politician in Texas as a speaker in the House of Representatives as well as the LT. Governor of Texas. It was well documented that he was the one responsible for getting a then young George Bush Jr. into the National Guard to avoid the draft. Also, a noted philanthropist Ben was an older guy, terribly nice and well mannered on the phone.

A client of mine for years, I was somewhat puzzled when he always insisted on paying with a credit card. What was it with these guys? I often wondered. Are they insane or just incredibly naive? Ben insisted on paying with his American Express card and was the only individual in the history of my service whom I accepted a credit card payment from at his insistence. I was always fearful of that money trail which would have meant the additional charge of 'money laundering' during my trial. Fortunately, my prudence paid off and I avoided that.

He was a darling Texan though, and often requested two or sometimes three girls at once. He really enjoyed watching the girls together before they would all join in with him. The girls always had very nice things to say about him. He treated them well which included buying them lunch and was not terribly demanding sexually. I was always glad to accommodate Ben whenever he called.

I phoned in and received his message.

"Hi, Ben. It's Sasha. How's the weather in Texas today?" I inquired.

"Well, Sasha, it's just great but I'm en route to Los Angeles now which is why I'm calling." he answered.

"Great! What can I do for you?"

"How about sending me three of your prettiest and tallest gals? You know my type" Ben teased.

And I sure did. He liked them tall, and young, blonde or brunette and busty. He was a waspy type.

I always thought the gals from Texas were absolutely stunning but just a bit different than the blondes found in Los Angeles. At the end of the day though a pretty gal is a pretty gal and usually pretty to most but some men could really be specific. Ben was pretty easy going.

"I'll be staying over at the Bel Air Hotel. I'd like them to meet me tomorrow afternoon in my room. We can start with some lunch" Ben suggested.

"So, three girls for you like last time? Will you be dining in or out? I asked.

"I think we'll stay in and they can order up whatever they like. I only have a little time though. Probably won't keep them more than two hours"he answered.

I began to flip through my notes in his file.

"I see. As I recall, Ben, you usually like the girls to put on a girlie show for you first which includes the girls having sex with each other before you join in. So, let's just make it $1000 per girl plus lunch. Total will be $3000. Are you still planning on using your American Express?" I asked.

"Yes, Sash, I am" Ben said.

I liked Ben and although I really didn't want to scare him, I did want him to be aware of the risks in paying for sex using a credit card.

"Ben, why do you do that? Don't you ever consider the repercussions of such actions?" I asked.

"Aw, Sash. Now, don't you go worrying your pretty little head about that" he said.

He had such a sweet southern accent.

"Just have the girls meet me at my room tomorrow at 3PM. I'll phone with my room number when I check in later today" he insisted.

"Alright then, Ben. As you like. I'll speak with you later" I said as we hung up the phone.

I was pretty familiar with his type of gal so I knew exactly who to phone.

"Beth, it's Sasha. Call me right back. I've got a booking for you tomorrow."

Beth was a pretty, tall, blonde, bi sexual gal and she was perfect to send to Ben. Since most gals usually had a girlfriend that they preferred doing bi sexual scenes with I always gave them the opportunity to choose a gal perhaps they might know first. If indeed she did not know anyone at that time, then I would send one of the other gals I thought she'd like. It was always a matchmaking game. Everybody wants a happy camper. I knew Ben would have a great time with my gals... he always did. Nothing wrong with that, just some good ole' harmless fun.

Beth and I played phone tag but eventually caught up.

"Hi, Beth, it's Sash. How are you?" I began.

"Great Sash! Got your message. What's up?" she asked.

"Well, I've got a bi scene for you tomorrow afternoon. Anyone in particular you'd like me to send for you?" I asked.

"Oh, yeah? cool! Hey, how 'bout that pretty girl of yours Emma? She's hot! I'd love to do her!"

"I'll call her and see if she's available" I offered.

"Sounds good. Who's the guy?"

"He's a real nice older client who's a high profile politician. Used to be the Lt. Governor of Texas and his name is Ben Barnes. Now here's the scene. He'll want to watch you and Emma together at first. Since he's older, he's not good for very long. Then he'll want the third girl to suck his cock while you and Emma are doing each other. Your time with him should be about an hour plus lunch. I'm not charging him for the lunch" I explained.

"So, he wants all three of us?!"

"Yup. The third girl I'm sending is not bi though. She's a real sweetie named Alana, a 6'0 tall blonde actress. It's $1000 for each of you. By the way, Ben pays by credit card."

"Wow! Sash, how will that work? We never take credit cards with you!"

The girls had never encountered a credit card transaction before and were well aware of my business policy of only dealing with cash.

"Not to worry. Just phone me with the credit card info when you get there. I'll pay out on it." I said.

This meant that I would collect Ben's funds by using his card but I would pay out the girls in cash.

"Got it. So, I can't make any moves on the other girl, huh?" she said teasingly.

"Now, be nice. She's totally straight but perfect for Ben."

"Oh, alright. When and where?"

I gave her the info.

"Ok. Tomorrow, 3 o'clock, Bel Air Hotel. You'll call me with the room number an hour before?" she asked.

"Yes. You all can order lunch first, but he doesn't have much time so don't order anything that'll take too long to prepare. I'll have Emma and Alana meet you in the room and settle up with all of you later. Call me and check in so I can run the card" I instructed.

"Cool. Then I'll wait for your call with the room number tomorrow" Beth finished.

"Right. Talk to you then" she said as we hung up the phone.

My next call was to Alana. She was unusually tall at 6' 0" and had mentioned having done some work in movies. But, with all the many Playmates and Penthouse Pets registered with my service, I didn't recognize her. She was a lovely gal who seemed like more the boyfriend type than the escort type to me. In fact, she was rarely available and made it clear that she did not want to be sent to anyone in the entertainment business.

"Alana, Hi. It's Sasha. I'm surprised to find you in" I began.

"Oh, Hi, Sasha. I'm having a bad day."

"What's the matter? Anything I can help you with?"

"I don't know. Just got a huge bill that I have no idea how I'm going to pay."

"Don't worry, dear. I've got some good news! I've got a great guy, a politician, anxious to meet you. It's a lunch gig with two other gals but you won't bother with them. You'll just be there to pay attention to my client."

"Really? How much?"

"You'll start with a quick lunch. He'll pay you $1000 for about an hour and a half; the half is for the lunch which I don't charge him for. He's a real sweetheart of a guy, too. The other two gals will be putting on a girlie show for him first."

"Okay. That sounds fine. This comes just in time. Thanks, Sasha."

"He pays by credit card but I'm cashing out for you. I'll meet you shortly after. You clear $600 on this."

"Sash, do you mind if I use another name? I'd like something that isn't so close to my own. Maybe, Lisa ?" she asked.

It was quite common for girls to use three or four different names at different times. I would remember to mark her down in the file as Alana/Lisa.

"Sure. That's fine. Just let Beth know that when you get there. She'll be in charge"

"Great! When and where?" she asked.

"3 o'clock tomorrow at the Bel Air Hotel. Can you find it?"

"I always have a problem with that Stone Canyon Rd. I'll just map quest it."

"Okay. Be ready at 2 30 because he's going to phone me with the room number" I instructed.

"Got it. I'll be ready" she finished.

"Okay, then. I'll speak with you tomorrow."

The following day I gave all three gals the information after hearing from Ben at our scheduled time. I waited for Beth to phone to give me the credit card info. If, for some reason, there was a problem with the card when I ran it I would have to handle that. But Ben was a good client and I had never had a problem before. Regardless, I still had to be aware of every possibility.

I wondered what was it that made Ben Barnes, a high profile politician, take these kinds of risks using escorts and paying by credit card? How many other services did he do this with? Did he need that kind of adrenaline rush taking these chances to get off?

Beth phoned me at 4:15 to check in and give me the credit card info which I ran. and then confirmed with no problem.

"It's all good, girl. Call me later when you're done and we'll meet to settle up" I said.

"Cool, Sash. Bye."

The girls knew the drill. They phoned upon arrival to check in. I would meet them shortly thereafter at the usual place to settle up. The usual place was an all night coffee shop.

It was around 5:30 that afternoon when I heard from her again.

"Hey, Sash. We're all done. Are you ready to meet?" she asked.

"I sure am. I can be at the coffee shop in about an hour. Are all three of you coming together?"

"Emma and I will be together, but Alana, I mean Lisa took off."

"Okay, then. I'll see the two of you over there."

I hung up to throw something on and grab my keys to run and meet the girls. That's always how it was; running to the recording studio, running to book the calls to pay for the studio time that always ran over budget, running to meet the girls. It was an insane schedule but somehow I managed to keep it all together. With homes to care for, 50 animals and Animal Control always threatening to take my animals, evading law enforcement, and so on and so forth. It was a grueling cycle that was spinning constantly with no end in sight. Somehow, I just kept on going.

Beth and Emma were both there when I showed up. We went in to the coffee shop and sat down at a booth.

"So, how'd everything go? Was Lisa okay?" I asked eager to here all the juicy details.

"She seemed fine, Sash. She clued me in on her name change. Emma and I started things off as you knew we would. We put on a real hot show for your client! He had his face right up there practically in our pussies! Then, after awhile your other girl, Lisa started playing with him, sucked his cock and he got off pretty quick" Beth said.

"Nice. So, did it seem like Ben liked Alana, I mean Lisa too?" I asked.

I would have to get used to calling her Lisa now and remember to note it in her file.

"Hard to tell, Sash. Emma and I were real wrapped up in each other. But there was no indication that he didn't like her. She was a real pretty girl. Tall, too!" she added.

"Yes, I know."

Most girls simply weren't that tall. In my entire history of dealing with hundreds of girls there were only a handful that were actually over 5' 9" and real attractive. Alana was one of them.

"Sounds like everything went well. Here's your money" I said as I handed them each their envelope.

"Yeah, thanks, Sash. It was cool. He was a real nice guy."

"Good, I'm glad you were happy. Please respect my rules about friendship outside of work" I reminded her.

I could tell this looked like a romance between these two gals waiting to bloom and at this point there was likely little I could do about it. But I mentioned it anyway. Emma was not available for solo bookings with male clients anyway. It always seemed to be a problem though, when two girls got together to compare notes. One always found out she hadn't been included on a particular job, etc., etc.

I decided to say goodbye and get on with my day. I still had to wait to settle up with Alana/Lisa and make sure she was okay too. She phoned later that evening… it seemed she had run off to a late afternoon audition.

"Hi, Lisa. Did everything work out okay?" I began.

"Oh, yes, Sasha. Thanks. It really helps with my rent. The guy was a doll and your girls were real nice. They seemed into each other" she said.

A good thing they left her alone.

"Great. When would you like to meet so I can give you your money?" I asked.

"I need to get it from you tomorrow for the rent but I might have a callback on this audition I went out on today. Can I phone you in the morning and let you know?"

"Sure thing. Call me anytime." I said.

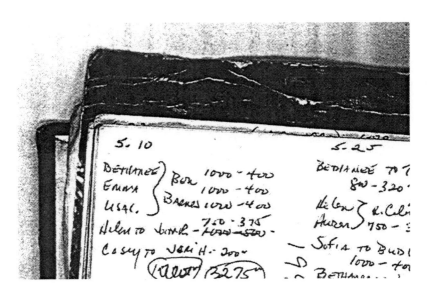

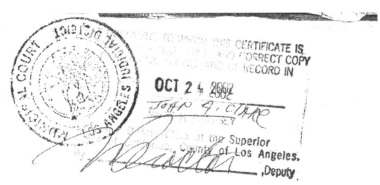

THE "BLACK BOOK" #1
BEN BARNES
OFFICIAL COURT SEAL OF AUTHENTICITY

Chapter 14: Jim Belushi

Jim Belushi first contacted me during the early 90's and he was an actor as well as the brother of famous actor John Belushi, who died of a drug overdose. I remember it like was yesterday. Jim was living on the Westside in Santa Monica on a street named Carmelita Way and had phoned to request a girl for he and his then girlfriend.

"Hi, Jim. It's Sasha returning your call."

"Hi, Sash. How've you been?"

Jim was always an upbeat kind of guy and always liked chatting with me. We actually ran into each other more than once at our local Mercedes dealer where we both purchased our cars. His was a black 600 SL.

"I'm great. Did you end up getting that beautiful black 600 SL I saw you looking at?" I asked.

"Oh yeah, runs like a dream! I love it."

"I bet! So, what can I do for you today? I got your page." I asked.

It was three o'clock in the afternoon.

"Well, I was looking for a girl to party with me and my girlfriend. She's gorgeous and wants a pretty girl as well" Jim explained.

"I see. No problem. Any particular type? Blonde, brunette, busty, short, tall, under 30, over 30?"

People could be extremely specific at times.

"No, not really. I guess a hot young blonde would be nice. Just make sure she's good with girls. My girl's a bit of a beginner so I need someone who knows what she's doing."

"No problem. I've got just the gal." I offered.

I actually had probably a hundred gals like that since most of the girls were more than willing to do a girl, girl threesome and often let me know it. Some girls employed with my service even specified that they were only available for that. But surely, this scenario would also include Jim's participation as I'd known from past bookings with him before.

"Sounds good. How much? The usual?" Jim asked somewhat teasingly.

"Yes, Jim. It's always $1500 for a girl, girl which includes you. Now, if you just want to watch and not have sex with my girl, then you can have it for a $1000" I answered.

"Now Sash, you know I can't guarantee that! It's too hot! No way! I'll pay the $1500" Jim laughed.

"Okay, fine. What time and where?" I asked

"My place tonight at 10PM. We'll be going out to dinner first."

I had Jim's home address in my file.

"Fine. Done. Have fun, Jim. I know that you will" I said.

"Thanks Sash. Bye" Jim said.

Walking over to my file marked "Girls' a real pretty young 22 year old bisexual busty blonde named Danielle came to mind. I gave her a call.

"Danielle, girl. It's Sash" I started.

"Hi, Sash. What's up?"

"I've got a good gig for you tonight with Jim Belushi, the actor. It includes a girl, girl scene with him and his girlfriend for $1500."

"Cool. What's his girlfriend look like? You know I can't take those fat ones!"

"Oh, no, honey. I'm sure she's a hottie. C'mon, he's got his own series now and seems to be raking it in so he can afford to be with anyone!" I replied.

"I know. Just joking. What should I wear? Will we be going out?"

"No, you're going straight to his place on the west side of town. I'd say jeans. You're only spending an hour. The session will include Jim after you two gals get started" I specified.

"Cool. That leaves me the rest of the evening if anything else comes in" she said.

Most of the girls could easily take two or three gigs in an evening as long as they weren't too demanding. We knew likely this would be an easy one. First off, Danielle loved girls and was a good little pussy eater. Second, Jim would probably get so turned on watching the two of them that it wouldn't take him long either.

"OK, girl. You're next up when something else comes in tonight. Here's the address" which I then gave to her. "Call me when you leave so I know you're available" I suggested.

"Will do."

Around midnight I received the call from Danielle.

"Hey, it's me. I'm done. Call me back" she said on my pager.

"Hey, Honey. How'd it go?" I inquired.

"Great! His girlfriend was real pretty. But Sash, whoever said she was a beginner? She ate my pussy like it was the last supper!"

"Really? He said she was!"

"Well, I find that hard to believe. Only thing was and may I be blunt?" she asked.

"Please" I said.

The girls knew they could always tell me anything.

"Well, she had one of those really hairy pussies. And you know how I hate to go down on a real hairy pussy! Someone ought to tell her to trim that bush! While I was lying down on my back with her eating my pussy, Jim began to fuck my mouth. He got off pretty quick" she said.

Actually, I hadn't known that but I sure knew it now. Just one more sexual detail for me to be aware of.

"Wow! Guess he likes that hairy type, huh?" I said.

"But anyway, it went really well. She's a pretty, slim blonde about 25. She wanted my phone number but I wouldn't give it to her" she said.

The girls knew the Agency Rule 'No phone number exchanges with clients.'

"Good girl. So, want to take something else and then we'll meet tomorrow to settle up?" I asked.

"You know I do" she confirmed.

I gave her the info and off she went...

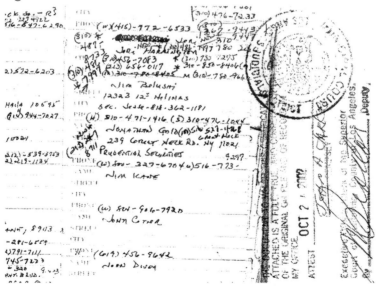

THE "BLACK BOOK" #2
JIM BELUSHI
OFFICIAL COURT SEAL OF AUTHENTICITY

Chapter 15: Designer Steve Madden

Steve Madden is a well-known fashion designer with a huge clothing empire. He was a client of mine who was particularly interested in anal sex. He would ultimately wind up doing time in prison for fraud but not before sending me his Vice President and some of his staff as well.

I had an adult film star named Erica who was an expert at this. Steve had grown quite fond of Erica. She had many talents in the sex arena that pleased him and showcased these talents in many of her adult films. Steve was a darling guy and would keep Erica for two hours, for which I charged him $4000. Anal play always got higher prices as most girls were not available to it and it required a girl who knew what she was doing. She was extremely comfortable with it and always said Steve was a perfect gentleman who treated her well often leaving her with a tip of $1000. He was actually very quiet most of the times we spoke which always led me to ask the questions.

I returned Steve's page immediately when he called asking for Erica. Fortunately, she was familiar with my Agency Rules and never slipped clients her phone number. It was always a concern when a client would request a particular girl too often. He could get attached and run off with a girl, which would mean I would lose not only a top girl, but also possibly a good client. I had spent years carefully screening thousands of calls a year that came through my office from clients and went to great measures to acquire a business clientele with those whom I knew would be top paying and treat the girls well. Good clients like that who could afford my high prices of $2000 per hour for anal sex were not standing on street corners. They were hard to find so I never wanted to lose one.

"Hi, Steve, it's Sash returning your call" I began.

"Hey, Sasha! How are you?"

"I'm great Steve. What can I do for you?"

"Well, I'd love to get together with my favorite girl, Erica" he said.

"No problem, Steve. She enjoys seeing you."

"I enjoy seeing her too. Sash, may I ask you something?" he inquired.

"Sure, Steve. Ask me anything you want."

"I know I usually give it to her in the ass. But do ya' think she'd mind if I asked her to stick her finger up my asshole too?"

"No, Steve. I'm quite sure she wouldn't mind. She's a well-known adult film star! Shall I mention it to her?" I suggested.

"Yes, I'd appreciate that" Steve said.

My clients knew they could request any sexual scenario they desired with me. My next call was to Erica.

"Hi, Erica. It's Sasha. How are you today?" I asked.

Erica was a busty exotic brunette who always knew exactly what she was doing. There was something very sensuous about her.

"I'm cool, Sash. What's up?" she answered.

"Well, Steve Madden called for you again. Tell me, as I've always wanted to ask you this, do you cum with him during anal sex?"

She responded immediately.

"Oh yeah! It's my favorite! I need the feeling of something in my ass."

"I'm assuming that you lube up pretty well first?" I questioned.

"Yup. It's important for sure. Why?" she asked.

"Just curious. You're one of a small group of gals I know who truly enjoy this kind of sex. You're actually famous for it in your movies!" I answered.

"Aaawww, thanks, Sash. It's cool. It's just one of those things that come really easy and natural to me. Plus, I like Steve. We party on his coke all night and sometimes I let him stick some of it up my ass, although it makes it kind of numb" she said.

"Interesting. Well, I guess we don't need to discuss too much here, huh?!" we laughed.

"Oh, I almost forgot. Steve requested that you stick your finger up his ass at your session today" I instructed.

"No problem, I'll have plenty of my lube with me. What time does Steve want to see me?" she asked.

"He mentioned Sunday afternoon around 3pm. Shall I get back to you with his info?"

"Yeah, call me later and leave it on my voice mail. I'll check in afterwards" Erica finished.

"Ok, then. Speak with you later" I said and we hung up the phone.

NAME Steve Madden
STREET 52-16 Barnett Ad. City 11105
CITY H (212) 254-9835
PHONE 718-446-18nn (800) 747-6233

STEVE MADDEN INSERT

ADDRESSES   ADDRESSES

NAME Sergio (D.H. Hope)   NAME Steve Ross
STREET   STREET 811 Roxbury
CITY (805) 279 5271 (m)   CITY (m)(310) 741-1300
PHONE (w)(310)291-4924 H.(805)290-2554   PHONE H 310-274-9132 (m)310-489-0266
NAME Seth Warshavsky   NAME Steve Scott
STREET 2000 1st Ave. #1404, Seattle 98101 STREET
CITY   CITY
PHONE (w)206-350-4444 H 206-269-0131   PHONE (w) 310-378-5591 (w)310-544-1401
NAME Steve Jones (310) 364-3357   NAME Sharga(B.H. Hotel) - R.S.Meridian
STREET 10001 Remsbury   STREET 10354 Wilshire #33   #506
CITY (Beverly Wilshire Wilshire 6) CITY 8760 Shoreham 360-9576
PHONE 310-274-4830 (m) 310-480-5290   PHONE 310-291-7030 (310)444-6431
NAME Sims (w)   NAME Steve Madden   (work) 11105
STREET   STREET 52-16 Barnett Ad. City 11104
CITY   CITY H (212) 254-9835
PHONE (M) 310-414-2546 P 587-0226   PHONE 718-446-18nn (800) 747-6233
NAME Maria Snipes   NAME Sonny (taylors Bar)
STREET   STREET
CITY (w)212-643-6633 Red:212-495-2524   CITY
PHONE (m)917-966-8866 (w)212-334-1236   PHONE (310)273-661K PH2
NAME Stephen (Barth)   NAME Jim (AA) Klutznik
STREET   STREET
CITY   CITY 30 W. 63 St. #15 H
PHONE (w)310-319-1204 (wn) 341-0033   PHONE (212) 956-4480
NAME Sam Gordon (w)   NAME Sidney Schlenker
STREET (m)(801)281-9198 (w)(801)841-8000   STREET (h) 310 718-701-9492
CITY House (801) 829-5896   CITY (w)(303)626-2636
PHONE 310-275-8634 (c)310-247-7800   PHONE (310) 478-5114

THE "BLACK BOOK" #2
STEVE MADDEN
OFFICIAL COURT SEAL OF AUTHENTICITY

126

PART FOUR:

"The Names" Pt 2

A *All of the client names presented herein were used as public record during my trial to aid in my prosecution and conviction. These names will include actual data from my trial marked as "exhibit # ". These exhibits are stamped with the official court seal taken from the Superior Criminal Court in Los Angeles, California determining their authenticity.*

You will see three sources of data retrieved from my personal belongings by law enforcement. They will include:

a) My actual "Black Book" #1 with appointments, names, and dollar amounts

b) My actual "Black Book" #2 with names, addresses, and phone numbers

c) A printout from my portable Wizard with names and phone numbers

Chapter 16: Gary & Jake Busey

Jake Busey was an up and coming actor whose father was Gary Busey. Although Gary had a long established career playing well known parts like Buddy Holly and starring in major films like Lethal Weapon with Mel Gibson, and Point Break with Keanu Reeves, it was actually his son that was my client. Jake was "client material" but I found that when it came to women and money they were nothing alike. Gary would never spend money on women like Jake did and you'd be lucky if he offered you a soda!

Years later, after dealings with Jake I was introduced to Gary socially through a friend. I never let him know when we spent time together that I had dealings with his son. Gary was the consummate professional when it came to his career but he was clueless when it came to how to treat the ladies.

He did have a nice big, fat dick though and had the potential to be a good lover when he wanted to. But definitely not a spender like his son. I liked Gary's eccentric nature, though.

I'll never forget my first date with him. We had met through a mutual gal pal friend when he first phoned me to chat. In the beginning we had long conversations on the phone and he would attempt to get philosophical with me.

"So, if you could be any animal which one would it be?"

It seemed rather silly and cliché but he appeared serious about it so I played along. He would play his guitar and serenade me for a while on the phone. I suppose it was his eccentricity that attracted me.

Then he came on with that whole "I'm born again" deal which almost completely scared me off for a variety of reasons. For one; I never cared much for extremist religious types and two; I was famous for running an illicit, scandalous, illegal business! So I knew likely it would clash with his so called religious beliefs. I never had any guilt nor felt remorse or regret for running my escort empire. I believed I had made all the right choices for myself at the time based on the options and things I was trying to accomplish. I never felt what I had done was criminally wrong. Immoral to some, perhaps, but I will never believe it is a criminal act. Nor did I feel it warranted prison time as a punishment. Although it was illegal by law, these were antiquated laws that were in dyer need of change; but not a criminal act because there never seemed to be a victim. I viewed it as servicing a very necessary need for people. So any lecture to me on my non-religious beliefs which I felt didn't apply, simply would not do.

But somehow I agreed to meet him when he suggested taking me out for dinner.

When Gary came to pick me up for our date I found him to be boyish, messy and unkempt but still somewhat attractive. I had just been released from prison and he was one of my first dates out of incarceration so quite frankly, anything would have looked good after being celibate for over two years. Since I was accustomed to the company of artistic eccentric types anyway, he was right up my alley. Until I got a taste of how rude he could be! We were on our way that evening when he said he wanted to stop off at his house in Malibu to pick up a jacket. As he had picked me up at my home in Beverly Hills it was a considerable distance from his home in Malibu and seemed a bit more like an excuse to get me quickly into his bed.

Curiosity had me continue to go along so we drove to his home in Malibu. Gary had a great big, black dog I took to right away and loved playing with. His home had a beautiful ocean view. It was sparsely decorated with a slight Native American flair.

However, I wasn't prepared for what happened next. Immediately after entering his home he jetted for his bedroom and shut the door! Without so much as offering me a drink or an explanation! Ten minutes, fifteen minutes, twenty minutes went by before I decided to knock on his bedroom door to see if everything was all right. I could hear that he was still on the phone.

"Gary, is everything ok?" I inquired politely.

"Yes, I'm on the phone" he answered in a rude tone.

"I can see that!" I returned curtly.

At that point I was turned off and wanted to leave, furious that I did not have my car. I did have my cell phone however, and considered just calling a cab.

"Gary, I can be at my place and be alone if I want that! I don't need to sit here and be alone!"

I stated firmly sounding agitated and fed up.

How rude! I was amazed at his lack of etiquette and bad manners. A few more minutes went by and he threw the door open as if angered by my disturbance of his telephone conversation.

"So, ready to go?" he asked.

Then he went on to act as if nothing had happened.

"Actually, I don't think we're getting off to a very good start and I think it's best if you just take me home!" I demanded.

I was really mad. He seemed shocked at this. He reached for the jacket we had stopped there for and we began to walk silently back to his car. It was a dirty red jaguar that looked like it was in dyer need of a wash. Too bad, I thought. There was still something rather cute about him. But I had a low tolerance for ill-mannered guys.

"Why don't we just go somewhere and sit down? I'm really

sorry and I'd like to take you to dinner and sit and chat and make it up to you" he offered apologetically.

He reminded me of a lost puppy. AGH! I knew this confused puppy was trouble but for some reason I decided to go along.

We drove to a lovely restaurant on the water near his place in Malibu. Everybody knew him. It seemed he had friends everywhere as people would shout out "Hey, Gary" as we drove by.

When we finally arrived at the restaurant we were seated immediately. During dinner he broke the ice and as we started to chat and I began to find him rather interesting to talk to. I told him that I was writing a book on my exploits as a Hollywood Super Madam.

"So, are you gonna 'blow the whistle?" he asked.

There was something really cute about the way he had said that.

"Maybe" I answered.

I still never led on that I had dealt with his son as my client. My goodness, if he only knew! Then he went into quite a bit about his being "born again" and it began to seem like he was going to try to save me, Oh, brother! I thought. Save me from what? I never believed I did anything wrong to begin with! Providing a very needed service to those who needed it. And since my girls were primarily adult film stars and actresses who were doing what they were doing anyway I never solicited them myself. They always approached me. I was just placing them in better environments, with better classes of people, for better money! But there was something terribly sweet about his wanting to save me.

Somehow, we made it through dinner. He seemed quite fascinated with the fact that I had just gotten out of prison for my Madam exploits. He told me he really felt bad and wanted to make me cum. I found his boyishness rather hot. We went back to his place and he led me into the bedroom where he immediately started to take off my pants and began to play with my pussy. He wasn't half bad either. Once I saw his big, fat cock I was a bit happier. Big, fat cocks always made me happy. He fucked me pretty good that night too, although he was not cooperative when it came to safe sex;

"Gary, I only have safe sex unless I'm in an exclusive relationship."

I immediately reached for one of the condoms from my Babydol Condom Compact carrying case. (www.babydol.com)

He was unsuccessful in his attempts to persuade me.

"Oh, c'mon; I'm clean."

"Ha! Now, how would I know that?! Besides, we both know you're quite the player."

Our romance continued and Gary would often call and ask me to come over and bring him his favorite Haagen-Dazs chocolate, chocolate chip ice cream. One ill-fated evening he showed me a photo of him in drag from a part in a movie he had done. He explained about how he was getting into his feminine side.

"I'm not real crazy about the way you look as a girl" I said.

"That really hurts my feelings. I had to get into my feminine side of this character for that film. Now, you've made me uncomfortable about it" he said.

Even though I was a fan of gay porn, somehow seeing him in drag really turned me off. I made some comment about it, which caused a huge altercation. We didn't speak again for some time…

His son, Jake Busey however, was another story. One of my Porn Stars, a hot brunette gal named Nina, had been fucking him regularly on her own when she called to tell me she was with Jake. Nina had phoned because they wanted another girl. Jake had done a few minor films so I was surprised to see he could actually afford the high prices for my girls.

Jake had actually been my client long before my meeting his dad, Gary. I remember when I first received that call from Nina.

"Sash, Hi. It's me. I'm at Jake's. He's in the bathroom but

wants to talk to you. I really need another girl here to help me with him" Nina said.

"Why?" I asked.

"He's really kinda' rough" she stated.

"How so?" I wondered.

"Well, his dick is a funny shape like a hook. He fucks me real hard… and, for a long time. I can't take him too long but he pays really well, so if you've got a girl who can take him you'll really make the money" she offered.

"Can he afford my $2000 for two hours prices?" I asked.

Jake was still in the bathroom and Nina was whispering while sneaking the call.

"Oh, yeah. No problem with the money. I'll put him on as soon as he comes out. Just send someone please!" she pleaded.

Gary would never spend money on the ladies and definitely not for sex!

"Alright, Sweetie. Don't panic. I'll send someone over who can help you handle him. I need to know though, is there anything dangerous about him?"

Safety was always a first priority when sending a girl.

"Is there anything else I should know?" I inquired.

"No, he's ok. Real good for the money. Just a rough fuck so make sure you send over someone who can take it" she added.

And with that, Jake came out of the bathroom and grabbed the phone.

"Hi, Jake. It's Sasha. Nina tells me you two would like a gal to join you? Nina will tell you I've got quite a few hot looking Porn Stars" I stated.

I had an ample supply and figured that was his type.

"Sounds good. Who ya' got and how much? Jake asked.

There didn't seem to be any time to send him to my site

to view photos of girls. Nina had sounded urgent. I began to rattle off some names of a few well-known Porn Stars whom he recognized immediately.

"You know, it's $1000 per hour minimum."

It was always my job to make sure business was clear even if someone else was sure about him.

"No problem. How soon can she get here?" he inquired.

"Right away. Are you out in Malibu?"

"Yeah. Is she far away? We don't like to wait" he added.

"I can have someone there in half an hour. I only accept cash, Jake" I said.

I needed to make sure everything was completely understood.

"Ok, send her over. I've got the $2000 for two hours. She better be hot!" he answered.

"She will be. Let me say goodbye to Nina."

Nina got back on the phone.

"Listen" I continued. "I'm sending someone over right away I know he'll love her so just hang in there" I assured her.

"Thanks, Sash."

Nina gave me the address and sounded relieved.

StarPeople

Matchmaker, matchmaker

Here's proof that there's somebody for everyone. **Jody "Babydol" Gibson**, the former madam who recently got out of prison, is crazy about **Gary Busey**. She was with a pal at Cafe Roma in BevHills when bad-boy Busey bounced in. Babydol begged her friend for an introduction. The friend warned her that Busey abused his wife, has done drugs and is totally wacky. But that only whet Babydol's appetite. P.S.: They've been inseparable ever since.

GARY AND I MAKE THE TABLOIDS;

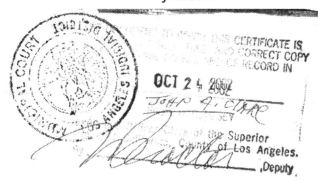

THE "BLACK BOOK" #1
JAKE BUSEY

Chapter 17: Barry Goldwater Jr.

B arry Goldwater Jr. was one of my earliest clients. He is the son of Senator Barry Goldwater and came from a lineage of politicians. After all, the Goldwaters are a legendary American family. From great grandfather, Mike Goldwater, to his famous father, Barry Sr., who was a CANDIDATE FOR THE OFFICE OF PRESIDENT OF THE UNITED STATES and the icon of Conservative politics in America, the Goldwaters have always earned the respect of their community, their state and their nation.

Barry Goldwater, Jr. was a Representative from California, born in Los Angeles, and was elected as a Republican to the Ninety-first Congress by special election to fill the vacancy caused by the resignation of United States Representative Ed Reinecke; but was an unsuccessful candidate for nomination to the United States Senate.

He retired from politics in 1993 and was a raving playboy with the ladies by the time I met him.

As I had not yet been open long enough to work out the 'kinks of running my service, I found myself a guest at his home in Studio City, Ca. one evening when I brought over one of my girls. He would be one of the very few clients ever to actually meet me as Madam Sasha.

Barry was particularly fond of large breasts. He seemed infatuated with a busty, petite, brunette employed with my service named Rebecca.

"Barry, this is a lovely home you have here" I said.

"Not as lovely as the girl you brought over with the big tits!" he exclaimed.

Clearly, he liked my choices.

"There's more where that came from" I offered.

Even though I had really just segued the modeling agency to an escort service, it seemed there was no shortage of available girls interested in partying with wealthy politicians.

"I hope so" he said and began to chase Rebecca around the house.

I turned to look around at all the political mementos that adorned the handsome walls of his living room. It was quite impressive. After a while when I was sure that Barry was happy with Rebecca, I picked up the envelope with my money Barry had left for me on the mahogany table that read "Sasha" and proceeded to find my own way out.

As I soon found out Barry was quite the womanizer. He had an insatiable appetite for petite, busty types and it seemed with all his wealth and prestige, he just couldn't get enough of them. He wasn't terribly generous and at first it was like pulling teeth getting him to pay. It was only a few days before I heard from him again.

"Barry, you've gone through just about every busty little babe I've got!" I said one day on the phone.

'Well, I guess that means you'll just have to find me more" he teased.

Those were the early days when my prices were a bit less. In those days you might be lucky enough to get a girl from me for an hour for $750. Since Barry was one of my first clients I hadn't yet discovered the potential of selling the idea of fantasy by featuring "title girls". It wouldn't be long though before my foray into casting would lead me to the Playboy

Playmates, which would alter the playing field considerably.

"Ok, then. There's someone that comes to mind that I think is perfect for you! She's a little brunette that's a 36EE with a gorgeous face. She just started with the service named Chloe. Shall I send her over?"

"Please."

"Will do, Barry. How long do you plan to keep her?"

"As long as I can hold out, Sasha" he teased.

"More than 2 hours?"

"That sounds about right. 36EE huh? Are they real?" he asked.

"No, but I've seen them and I have to say she's got one of the best boob jobs I've ever seen! She insisted I touch them and I was amazed at how soft they were! And she's so tiny. Can't be more than a size 2 "I said.

"Wow! Please send her as soon as possible! I'll pay whatever you want!"

That was the beginning of the realization that an affluent man would pay anything, or practically do anything to satisfy his appetite for the gal that was his type. I decided to test the waters a bit.

"How's $2000 for 2 hours?" I suggested.

"Fine" he agreed.

That was the last of my $750 deals.

.

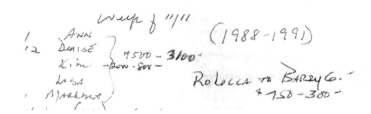

THE "BLACK BOOK" #1
BARRY GOLDWATER JR.

OFFICIAL COURT SEAL OF AUTHENTICITY

Chapter 18: Martha Stewart's CEO Charles Koppelman

Charles Koppelman may now be CEO of Martha Stewart Enterprises, but at the time he was my client he still owned a record company famous for handing Vanilla Ice and the Wilson/Phillips sisters. A label known as SBK records which he later sold for millions. It might have been around the time of this sale that I received this call from him as it seemed he wanted to celebrate some good fortune by taking eight of my girls for himself and his staff to party with in Palm Springs. He was also married to Coco Koppelman, a NY socialite often written about in the papers. Charles had phoned me to discuss which girls from my web site he would like me to send for the big party in Palm Springs to celebrate.

"Hi, Charles. It's Sasha returning your call" I began.

"Hi, Sash. How's business? Good?" he inquired.

"Yes, but not quite as good as yours I'm sure" I laughed.

Everyone knew about the big sale of his record company as it was in all the papers. Charles was an older guy and very polite even if he was a big business mogul. The truth was I had just finished recording my album that I had invested upwards of $150,000 in and was simply dying to send it to him. But alas, I was well aware that after leading my double life as

I had been doing for years as Babydol, recording artist and Sasha, Super Madam of the escort empire it would be impossible that he would even believe I could really be these two very contrary people. Let alone perform musically as Babydol, after negotiating business with me for years on sex as Sasha. The escort business was a ruthless one and it required a certain kind of thinking. If it were that easy, everybody would be doing it. So I had to refrain from ever mixing my two lives and continued to keep things completely separate.

"Yes, Charles, business is great, thank you. What can I do for you today?" I continued.

"Well, I need eight of your finest for me and my staff. We're all going to fly on my private plane to Palm Springs and celebrate for the weekend.

"Congratulations, I read about it in Variety. My, that sounds wonderful Charles" I said.

Of course my mind was already adding the numbers on what I'd make with eight girls for the weekend, and which girl I would place in charge to handle the money for me. With my high prices I knew we were talking about at least $90,000 dollars total here, my cut of which would be $36,000. The math took little effort as I began to calculate the numbers easily in my head since in those days I was used to doing this on a daily basis. That was a lot of money for some girls to be responsible with so I had to put someone in charge that I knew I could trust. I decided on my gal, Bobby, a hot busty blonde who worked for me many times on deals much larger than this so I was confident she'd be fine to handle things.

"I've got a few new hot busty blondes you boys would have some fun with. And they really love to party. I just need to know some specifics from you. Will you have eight separate rooms as in one guy per girl; or are you planning on switching off girls and guys?" I inquired.

Switching off meant that perhaps the girls would be with more than one guy, each which would determine the outcome of my price.

"I'm sure they'd enjoy a little dance and girlie sex show first of course. But will all of you be choosing and pairing off one on one?" I inquired.

There was always a possibility that a hot girl might seem attractive to more than one guy and these things might happen even unexpectedly. Sometimes, one girl might be with up to three different men. My job was to prepare the girls for everything.

"Gee, can't really say for sure, Sash. But I think each guy will pick one gal and we'll end up pairing off" he answered.

"I see. No problem with that. Are you thinking perhaps they join you from Friday night to return Sunday?" I asked.

"Something like that. Depends on how much fun we're all having Sash. But I do need my staff back in the office by Monday morning... especially, my attorney. You know how persuasive your girls can be" he chuckled.

"I sure do and it's no accident, Darling" I laughed. "Then let's just make it a flat $10,000 per girl and you boys have the girls back by Sunday evening. One guy per girl though" I confirmed.

It was usually $5000 per day but I knew Charles would likely take them out and show them a great time and tip well as he had done so in the past. Plus, he was a good client so it wouldn't hurt to cut him a little slack.

"Also, Charles, are you interested in any beautiful Asian, exotic or Afro American gals? Anyone want any particular type?" I inquired.

"As a matter of fact, one guy has a thing for Asian gals but she has to have big tits" he said.

"No problem, I've got a gorgeous busty Asian gal who was Miss Hawaii. She's tall, elegant, and great company. Her photo is on my site. Look at # 11" I offered.

Having photos available for clients to view beforehand was an idea I came up with early in my escort service career as I learned it accomplished several things;

1) It discouraged the possibility of a client sending a girl away claiming she was not his type; and

2) It offered the client the luxury of choice.

Hard to believe now that when I first came up with the idea in 1990 of featuring models for hire as escorts on my web site that absolutely no one else was doing it! And now, sex is all over the Internet.

Technology had come a long way.

"Sounds great, Sash. No time to view photos right now but I'll have some of the guys take a peek later. We're all going in to a big staff meeting soon. Besides, I trust your taste" Charles answered.

My clients usually did which explains why most of them remained with me for up to ten years.

"If you have a few of your Playboy Playmates available I'd really like that too" he added.

"Absolutely fine, but you know that the title girls always get more" I said.

This was because whenever a gal appeared in Playboy, Penthouse, adult films, or beauty pageants she could easily command higher prices making her a "title girl" as I affectionately named them. After my foray into casting for Playboy and Penthouse, as well as packaging adult films, it would soon be the only sort of girls employed with my service. I learned quickly the concept of selling fantasy and realized that affluent men would pay any amount of money to meet the girl of there dreams they'd seen in magazines or movies.

"It would be at least $15,000 per girl for a Playmate or adult film star for the weekend" I said.

"Well, Sash, how about two Playboy Playmates? I'll pay the $30,000 for that one. The guys would really love that and a girlie sex show too. The Playmates will be for my attorney and me. I need to keep him real happy," Charles added.

"Smart thinking, Charles. It's a good idea to keep your attorney happy. That brings the total to $90,000 dollars. $30,000,

144

for the two Playmates, plus $10,000, per girl for the six remaining girls" I said. .

My 40% cut would be $36,000 just on this job.

"Fine" Charles answered.

"Alright, then. What I'd like you to do is place all the $90,000 in one envelope and give the whole thing to a beautiful blonde named Bobby. She'll pay the girls and it will be easier this way" I suggested.

This meant that Bobby would be holding $36,000 of my money after paying the girls.

"No problem, Sash. I'll do that. A limo will pick up all the girls and bring them to meet us at my private plane. I'll phone you back and you can tell me where to send the driver" Charles offered.

I admired the way he always conducted things in such a first class manner. He had style.

"Sounds good" I said. "Call me back" as I hung up the phone.

The rest of the hour would be spent on gathering together the eight girls for the trip.

My first call was to Bobby the one who I was going to trust with my money. The next job was to choose the two Playmates. As my service employed many of the Playboy Playmates I wasn't terribly concerned. I had expected they would all be ready, willing and anxious to make that kind of money, let alone fly to Palm Springs on a private plane for dinner and have such a trip. It wasn't too hard to find eight hot girls as I had over three hundred listed with my service to choose from. I phoned all eight girls and outlined the scenario and the way it seemed like the evening would go. Then, I called Charles back to give him the details of where to pick up all the gals.

"Hi, Charles. No problem, I've got you covered" I assured him.

"Great, Sash. I know I could always count on you" he added.

"Have a good time" I finished.

"You can be sure I will."

The gals were confirmed and the booking was in. I began to make all the needed notes in Charles' file. It was usually my policy to have the girls phone and check in upon arrival so I knew all was going well. I remained seated close to my pagers and phones.

The page came in at precisely 10 pm that Friday evening.

"Hey, Sash. It's me, Bobby. We're all here and I've got the envelope. I'll be sure to keep my eyes on my bag" she assured me.

Bobby was a real smart gal, which is what I liked about her. I didn't expect to hear from her again until her return home on Sunday.

I awoke early that Sunday morning ready to receive the call from Bobby about how the weekend with Charles had gone. It was hot in Palm Springs and I was sure Charles had kept them all real comfortable in a private suite at the best five star hotel. Knowing him, it was likely he had taken the entire floor.

"Hi, it's me. We're all back and we had a blast! I've got your money. Call me" was the message she left.

So I called her.

"Hi, Gorgeous. How'd everything go?" I began.

"Smooth as silk! His private plane was beautiful and we started the evening off in flight with some Crystal champagne. Then, he checked us in to a lovely five star hotel in Palm Springs where the girls and I changed into some evening clothes for dinner. He took us out for a lavish seafood dinner and we all got smashed before heading back to the hotel. We were a large group. Like ten guys and eight girls" Bobby said.

"Really? How did that work out? Did someone take two guys or were two of the guys left out?" I asked.

"No way! It was like one big orgy! Everybody was fucking and sucking everybody! I eventually ended up with his attorney in another suite towards the end of the evening. But at first, it seemed like it was like three girls with one guy, or sometimes it seemed everyone was switching off with everyone. I think some guys also enjoyed watching all the hot action. Your two Playmates started things off with a dance and put on a real hot girl on girl sex show. They began kissing and making out with each other. Then, one girl started sucking on the other's nipple. They brought out their strap-ons and fucked each other bumping and grinding in front of us all! It was really hot! After the major orgy it seemed like people just started pairing off. Charles took all the suites; we had the whole floor to ourselves. Everybody seemed real happy as they said on the way home" she finished.

"Really?" I asked." Did any of you receive any tips?"

"Actually, his attorney tipped me $500, and I think some of the girls got the same. Charles ended up in a room with the two Playmates. It was really hard to keep track Sash"she said.

I realized it was an almost impossible scenario to control.

"As long as the girls were happy. Was everyone paid?" I inquired.

"Oh, yes. I took care of that plus I've got your money. We had a great time! When do you want to meet to settle up?" she asked.

"Tonight if possible" I suggested.

After all, she was holding $36,000 of my money.

"Ok, I can meet you in a little while, say 9 pm?" she offered.

The girls knew that if they wanted to keep steady employment with my service, getting me the money as quickly as possible would insure their booking for the next time.

"Good. I'll see you over at the coffee shop and we'll chat more then," I said.

"The usual place?" she asked.

"Yes. See you there".

The usual place was an all night coffee shop I used to meet the girls. One of my earliest lessons in the escort business was to never allow girls to come to my home. This made it harder for law enforcement to find out where I lived. Just one more of the many, many buffers I had come to create over the years to insure my safety.

Bobby was waiting there at 9 pm when I showed up. We sat down at a booth and she handed me the envelope. I immediately counted the money to make sure.

"It's all there, Sash" she said.

"I know, honey. Force of habit" I consoled her. "Be right back."

I excused myself to walk up to the ladies room so I could count the money. I was quite used to counting cash and had a particular way of licking my fingers before handling the bills like they do in the movies. I loved counting money; 34,000, 35,000, 36,000, all in crisp $100 bills. After I was sure it was all there I returned to join her at our table so we could finish our chat.

"So" I continued. "What was his attorney like?" always mindful to get the juicy details.

"Well, he was a Jewish guy. Real nice. Not really into fucking and basically just wanted to eat my pussy all night! He was pretty good at it too, so I can't say I had a problem with that" she said as we both laughed. "He wanted my telephone number and offered to send me flowers but I told him about your policy. No exchanging numbers with clients."

The girls knew all too well that if they ever wanted to work for my service again following the Agency Rules was a must.

"I couldn't take him for very long, Sash. He talked too much" she said.

"I understand. That can really be annoying! But you know there are worse ways to make $6000 for a weekend party in Palm Springs" I teased.

That was what her "end" came to; it was $10,000 less my 40% cut which equaled $6000 for her. The other two Playmates would clear a bit more at $9000 each.

I took out $500 and handed it to her.

"That's for taking care of the money" I said..

I figured it was sort of an incentive.

"Aawww, thanks. You know it! I think Charles was real happy too. Plus, I noticed your Asian girl was gorgeous and that guy really liked her" she added.

"Good" I said.

"Hey, Sash, keep me in mind for the next one, huh?" she asked.

"You bet I will."

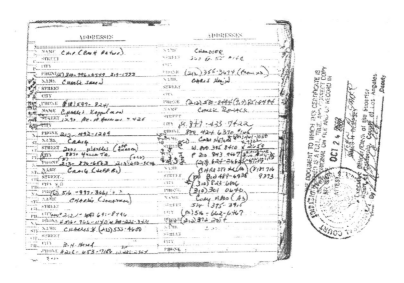

THE "BLACK BOOK" #2
CHARLES KOPPELMAN
OFFICIAL COURT SEAL OF AUTHENTICITY

NAME *Charles Koppelman*
STREET *1290 Ave. of Americas " 42F*

INSERT

Chapter 19: The Sultan of Brunei
Richest Man in the World

Many of the most lucrative meetings I negotiated in my service actually lasted a very short time since that gentlemen knew the moment he saw the girl whether he was interested in keeping her for the appointment or not. I can remember my client, the Sultan of Brunei.

Although recognized by Forbes as the richest man in the world with a fortune estimated at $40 billion dollars, Brunei is actually less than the size of Delaware, and is located on the island of Borneo in Southeastern Asia bordering on the South China Sea and Malaysia.

The Sultan has several wives as he never tired of the company of beautiful women and had them sent from all over the world. He had a unique sort of interview for applicants fortunate enough to be granted entry into his lavish and opulent existence, which would initiate in London, England during the time he was my client. They were flown in and sent to the Dorchester Hotel also owned by the Sultan. We would wait for the first call that would determine their fate, which included the opportunity to make millions of dollars. That call would lead to further instructions to meet a Mr. Ball, the gentleman in charge of screening the girls. He would arrive to meet them often spending less than ten minutes and then exit without saying a word or giving any indication as to what he thought. The girls were paid $14,000 per week just for this screening. I would then receive further instructions soon after as to whether they would be flying on to Brunei to meet the Sultan and the possibility of earning a fortune of money which would include $25,000 per week to remain in Brunei, or simply take the $14,000 and return home. Mr. Ball knew in thirty seconds whether a girl was a suitable choice based on her appearance. They had a fondness for young American girls and would demand to peruse their passport for proof of age. Sometimes, he would suggest perhaps a gal might be right to meet the Sultan's brother Prince Jeffri instead known as the bad boy of the family. This outing would on rare occasions include sex with Prince Jeffri but never ever included sex with The Sultan. Either way, the girls were paid the same $25,000 per week. And usually there was no sex involved!

The Sultan enjoyed collecting a bevy of the most beautiful young women from all over the world. Although he enjoyed all different types he was especially partial to beauty pageant winners and well-known American actresses from television or movies and Playboy Playmates. They would be all housed together on a lavish compound in Brunei. No men were allowed except for the workers. Here he would gather as many as 500 women at one time! Meow...

The girl's only requirement was to be on call and available to attend these huge galas that he would arrange and insist the girls get all dressed up for. The compound consisted of 1788 rooms including a large disco, and banquet hall large enough for 4000 guests where he held the galas. With 267 toilets, all of the faucets in the sinks were made of solid gold, and they matched the opulent solid gold dome that rested atop the ornate 400 million dollar Palace, thought to be larger than the Vatican and considered the most lavish palace in the world.

An early success story of mine with The Sultan and his brother Jeffri was with a lovely exotic looking Moroccan gal named Romani, who resembled the well known model from the early 90's named Yasmeen. A stunning gal with a slim figure and an absolutely gorgeous face there was a natural elegance to her. Romani was completely destitute when she came to me without even the use of a car and was quite upset about having rented a room in the palatial home of some dirty old man she complained about in Bel Air, a wealthy land developer named Don Tanner.

He had offered her a place to stay but never stopped chasing her around harassing her for sex, contributed no money towards her needs, took her rent money, and did not even offer this gorgeous lovely gal the use of one of his many cars. I had my own run in with Don in the past when he had contacted my service at one time for a girl. So I knew exactly what she was going through and was most sympathetic based on my previous experience with him. Don was partial to a gal he had seen on my web site named Brandy, a beautiful busty blonde whom he phoned me raving about wanting to meet.

When we chatted on the phone I clearly explained my prices, which he agreed to. We then set a meeting for him to meet Brandy at the lovely Bel Air Hotel as he lived nearby on several acres of his palatial Bel Air grounds. However, when Brandy showed up Don was not present. Instead, she was greeted by an older gentleman named Gary, a friend of Don's. He claimed that Don was running late but was on his way and suggested they proceed inside to the lounge area for a drink and wait.

The lounge in the Bel Air hotel was quite elegant, and furnished with beautiful couches along with a lovely fireplace, which provided a darling ambiance; a very "old money" sense of style. They sat down and ordered two cappuccinos.

Brandy phoned me to check in and update me always mindful that time was money. After about forty-five minutes though, she phoned back to inform me that Don had still not showed up and asked what she should do. I instructed her to please put Gary on the phone.

"Hi, Gary. It's Sasha. Brandy tells me you've been waiting for forty-five minutes for Don. Is everything alright?' I inquired.

"Well, he's on his way" he replied.

"I see. At this point though, I'm going to have to ask you to pay her for the first hour as she has clearly been sitting there taking up her time" I demanded. "Otherwise, I'll have to tell her to leave."

I was rather surprised to then discover that not only did Gary have not have any money to pay my girl, but he then tried to stick her with the check for the drinks! I immediately phoned the Concierge whom I knew and instructed Brandy to leave at once. Fortunately, I knew all the Concierges at the major hotels as many were on my payroll. They were an asset and kept me informed when wealthy clientele checked in requesting their company.

So much for wealthy millionaire land developers...

I decided to send Romani to Brunei. Although it seemed she was not the Sultan's type after the initial meeting in London took place, they did feel she might be suitable for his brother, Prince Jeffri, who indeed took a liking to her. She remained for three years in Brunei with Prince Jeffri ultimately becoming his personal assistant. I'm quite sure she made millions.

Another success story with the Sultan was with a gal in my service named Donna. When Donna first came to me she was 19 yrs old and flat-chested. But she was a 5' 8"blonde with a pretty face. I asked her what it was she wanted and she answered emphatically:

"I want to get my breasts enlarged, get a nose job, and appear in Playboy magazine."

I helped her make the money which led to her breast enlargement and nose job, followed by an appearance in Playboy magazine. She couldn't be happier and I must admit she looked gorgeous after the surgery. The average duckling had become the beautiful swan right before my eyes.

She went on to Brunei where she was chosen to stay with the Sultan. During her stay there Donna would phone me with stories of all the catfights the girls were getting into. Several months turned into the first year, and she phoned to say she had become the Managing Director of the girls and their social events there. Normally, this would have provided a winning formula for me to continue sending girls but an unfortunate high profile scandal took place shortly thereafter with a Miss America.

"Sasha, it's Donna. I'm calling you from the Sultan's Palace in Brunei!" she said.

"Wow! The reception is pretty darn good! What's happening? Are there a lot of other American girls there?" I asked.

"No, there was a huge scandal! Didn't you see it in the papers?"

Apparently, this Miss America was not happy and caused a huge fuss in the press which most believed was simply an attempt to garner more publicity. According to Donna, all this pageant winner was required to do was parade around the compound with her Miss America sash on. But, she felt she was being mistreated. In all my years dealing with The Sultan and the sending of many, many girls there I had never once heard anything about anyone ever being mistreated. In fact, they were informed that they were free to leave anytime they wanted. But for $25,000 per week to do nothing but get dressed and attend private galas, who would want to?! Because the Sultan loathed publicity and scandal the decision was made to cease sending any more American girls.

Except for Donna who remained there.

During the start of her second year there she phoned to tell me how she had managed to get close to a million dollars into the United States without being taxed on the money, or having to pass through customs upon entry into the United States. I always had these discussions with the girls about this very thing. My advice was to declare the money and just pay the taxes on it. It was illegal to try to get more than $10,000 into the country undeclared and if found, in addition to being arrested, the money they just made would be confiscated and taken from them. Some girls however, did not heed my advice and were ultimately arrested. The Sultan and his organization offered little assistance with this dilemma preferring to leave all advice and decisions the sole responsibility of the girls. But, on this particular day Donna had phoned to tell me that the Sultan had flown her and all her cash into the United States on his 400 seat jumbo jet private plane, which also had the solid gold faucets, turquoise leather furniture, and exquisitely designed matching end tables of lapis lazuli trimmed in gold.

"Sash, it's me, Donna"

"Hi, Gorgeous. Are you okay?" I asked

"Oh, yeah. The Sultan just flew me in on his private plane from Brunei! He managed to get me straight through customs because of his diplomatic immunity. I have over a $1,000,000 in cash on me right now!" she said.

"Get out! What are you going to do?" I inquired curiously.

"Well, we're on our way to pick up my mom. He's treating us to a few days in Vegas. He gave me $25,000 spending money for mom and I to enjoy ourselves with. My mom says she wants me to pay the taxes on the $1,000,000 just to be on the safe side" she said.

"Your mom's right, Donna. Do it".

"Yeah, I guess. Well, I gotta go now. I'll catch up to you later" she finished.

With his diplomatic immunity they whizzed by customs and she was able to get all the money into the USA undeclared!

A fascinating story, she remained there for several years flying back and forth and at last count had made several millions of dollars.

THE "BLACK BOOK" #1
THE SULTAN OF BRUNEI

Chapter 20: Sex Pistol's Steve Jones

Steve Jones was the guitarist for the famous punk group the Sex Pistols with Sid Vicious and Johnny Rotten. The Sex Pistols were only together for two years in the late 70's but they managed to change the face of popular music.

When he first contacted me it was considerably later in his career. He had now gotten a bit older, perhaps in his forties. I found him to be a darling and generous guy, usually well mannered often referring to me as "Yes, Love"… very English.

"Hi, Steve. What's up?"

"My dick" he said.

Men could be rather crude when horny.

"So, Love. Who've we got for me tonight?" he would begin.

"Steve, you know I always have whatever it is you want" I assured him.

His preference was for me to send him a gal that could role play like The Daddy's Girl.

"Ah, Love you know what I like. Someone young and pretty, who can sit on my lap. I'd like her to have a nice bum too. Maybe she can wear one of those real short skirts with little girl socks. Huh, Sash?"

"Yes, Steve..I have a lovely little girl for you. She'll sit on your lap and call you daddy for as long as you like."

"Really? Aaahh, Love, I'm getting hard just thinking about it. What does my little girl look like?" he asked.

"She's about 5'4", with long blonde hair and big blue eyes. Her name is Darla. Great little ass, too."

"She sounds terrific, Love. How 'bout sending her my way tonight, say 8 o'clock?"

"Sounds good, Steve. Shall we assume the usual? $2000 for the two hours?"

"Yes, Love."

"Great. Have fun."

Steve never seemed to change his desire for this type and often the girls would tell me how he enjoyed chasing them around the room. Hence the "cat and mouse" game He was adamant that they be dressed in something resembling a little girl's outfit with anklet socks and sneakers, and insisted they call him Daddy. He was also at times turned on to the Bad Little Girl, as well as the Good Little Girl, which would include giving the girls a light but innocent spanking on the butt. The girls always said he had a big cock and enjoyed penetration with them for a considerable amount of time. He would keep them for several hours which he never had any problem paying for. The good thing was since wardrobe played a huge part of his visual turn on, much of the time I sent him girls in their late twenties who he was convinced were still in their teens. As long as they dressed the part and appeared youthful he was happy.

NAME Steve Jones (310) 264-3357
STREET 10001 Reevesbury
CITY [Benedict 2½ mi. to West Wanda Ct]
PHONE# 310-274-4030 (M) 310-480-

STEVE JONES INSERT

ADDRESSES		ADDRESSES	
NAME Sergio (B.H. Hotel)		NAME Steve Rex	
STREET		STREET 811 Roxbury	
CITY (805) 279-5277 (m)		CITY (m) (310) 741-1300	
PHONE (w)(310) 281-2924 H.(805) 290-2594		PHONE # 310-274-9133 (w) 310-489-0866	
NAME Seth Warshavsky		NAME Steve Scott	
STREET 2000 1st Ave., #1404, Seattle 98101		STREET	
CITY		CITY	
PHONE (m) 206-330-4444 H 206-269-0131		PHONE (H) 310-278-5551 (c) 310-544-1401	
NAME Steve Jones (310) 264-3357		NAME Shgal B & Aaron - C Smeghow	
STREET 10001 Reevesbury		STREET 10354 Wilshire #33 506	
CITY [Benedict 2½ mi. to West Wanda Ct]		CITY 8760 Shoreham 360-9276	
PHONE 310-274-4030 (M) 310-480-		PHONE 310-274-7030 (310) 360-2431	
NAME Steve (L.)		NAME Steve Madden Long Island	
STREET		STREET 52-16 Barnett Rd, City 11104	
CITY		CITY A (718) 254-9835	
PHONE (M) 310-614-2546 P 592-0226		PHONE 718-444-1810 (800) 747-6233	
NAME Marvin Singer		NAME Sammy [Address Book]	
STREET		STREET	
CITY (212) 643-6632		CITY	
PHONE (M) 917-861-8866 (212) 334-1731		PHONE (310) 273-668X #42	
NAME Stephen (B.H.H.)		NAME Sun (AA) Klutznik	
STREET		STREET	
CITY		CITY 30 W. 63 St. #15A	
PHONE (c) 310-319-1704 (800)		PHONE (812) 956-4460	
NAME Skip Corradi (w) 891-0022		NAME Sidney Schlenker	
STREET (805) 281-4198 (w) (805) 891-8002		STREET (R) (310) 778-901-9492	
CITY Hawaii (808) 889-5286		CITY (310) 326-2236	
PHONE 310-275-0624 (c) 310-247-7800		PHONE (210) 278-5114	

THE "BLACK BOOK" #2
STEVE JONES
OFFICIAL COURT SEAL OF AUTHENTICITY

Chapter 21: Producer Jon Peter's Stunts Like "Batman"

Jon Peters was a hairdresser turned movie mogul once he joined creative forces with Peter Guber. As a team they produced many successful hit movies that earned them millions of dollars. During the years he was my client he would have the girls visit him at his palatial estate in Beverly Hills. At the time, Jon was also in the middle of a hot romance with the famous model Vandela, as well. It showed as his preference was for tall, blonde, slim model types.

He had mentioned that he was particularly sensitive about paying the girls. I actually believed him when he said that he just felt so uncomfortable about giving the girls their money. So, I offered to run him a tab of $3000 which I had never done before and went against my better judgement by doing so. This meant he had an account with me whereby he could run up to this amount with girls, and I would pay out the girls on it. When it got to $3000 I would go and collect it from him. Really though, this tab only amounted to a few dates at a time at my prices.

In the beginning it seemed to work out quite well and made Jon feel better which also gave me more of his business. This proved to be short lived for it wasn't long before he attempted to cheat me on the funds. It was on one such afternoon that I can remember driving over to his large estate to receive my envelope with the $3000 in it as I had done so many times before. On this particular day however, it seemed the money was considerably short. I phoned Jon from my car immediately.

"Jon, there seems to be a problem as all the money isn't in my envelope" I began.

Jon was not the least bit surprised and answered me instantly as if he expected I'd be calling.

"Sash, come on back" he said.

"Jon, why did you short me on the money?" I demanded.

Clearly I sounded irate.

"Gee, Sash, I just wanted to see if you were paying attention" he answered sarcastically.

This of course angered me and meant that I was forced to turn the car around and drive all the way back to get the matter corrected. During my reign as the Hollywood Super Madam I had guys on my payroll equipped to handle matters that involved collecting financial balances of monies owed to me. But it was the mere audacity of his doing this after I'd been nice enough to extend my generosity towards him that offended me most.

"Jon, why wouldn't I be paying attention?" I answered. "This is my business! Don't you pay attention to your finances and the amounts of debits and costs in your line of work? Obviously, I need to remind you that it's a luxury for you to have this tab with me since I don't do this with anyone else!"

It took me awhile to realize that the reason for the tab with me had little to do with Jon being over sensitive about giving girls money as he would have liked me to believe in the beginning. The real deal was that Jon Peters felt that young, beautiful, nubile girls should be grateful just to be with him because he was a rich and famous movie producer. It seemed he really resented compensating them at all. Granted, he was certainly attractive and I understood his need for this sort of ego gratification. But, he needed to realize that it was the "convenience factor" that he was paying for. To have young, beautiful, nubile girls available to service him at his beck and call was a luxury.

"But Jon, most of my clients are some of the biggest and most successful producers and directors in town! They have no problem understanding that gorgeous girls have better things to do with their time then to come over on a whim at their convenience to entertain them for free!."

Apparently, Mr. Peters was under the misconception that he was the only crap game in town. Needless to say that was the end of my dealings with Jon Peters.

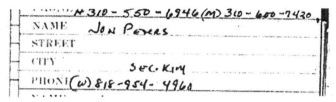

INSERT FROM THE "BLACK BOOK" #2
JON PETERS

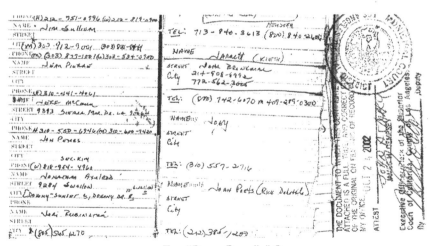

THE "BLACK BOOK" # 2
JON PETERS
OFFICIAL COURT SEAL OF AUTHENTICITY

Chapter 22: Robert Evans "Godfather" of Kink

Robert Evans was the legendary producer of movies like The Godfather, Chinatown, Popeye, Love Story, and countless others when he was the President of Paramount Pictures. I first met Robert as a friend socially when my Billboard sat high atop Sunset Blvd as Babydol. He had been kind enough to be a part of a short film I made about it called "The Making of a Billboard on Sunset" and agreed to grant me an interview in his lavish and palatial Hollywood mansion in Beverly Hills located behind the Beverly Hills Hotel. I found him to be a very giving and generous friend and we would spend hours together in the huge movie room of his home chatting and laughing.

He invited me to lovely lunches with people like high profile attorney Robert Shapiro, as well as some of the extravagant parties he often had in his home.

It was a few years before I would let him in on my "double Life" as a Hollywood Super Madam but when I did, he found my life fascinating and thought it should be a movie. His exact words were;

"Baby, your life is like a movie. The only problem is you don't have Act 3."

I came to find Act 3 years later after my arrest.

After I let him in on my deep dark secret he became my client. In the beginning, Robert was a terrific client. He was handsome and lived the life of a movie star in the truest sense. All the girls loved him and he was a real "ladies man". His palatial estate in Beverly Hills lay nestled behind the Beverly Hills Hotel. Here, I would join him at the lavish parties he would host with it's elegant black bottomed pool surrounded by a beautiful spray of shooting fountains. All of this was spread out amongst the perfectly manicured grounds.

The inside of his home was just as glamorous too, with all of his memorabilia from many of the legendary films he produced. Letters and personal photos of his movie star friends like actor Jack Nicholson, or director Francis Ford Coppola, sat framed atop the gorgeous black baby grand piano which stood commanding attention in the formal dining room. Robert would look simply stunning in his cream colored slacks complemented by the pale yellow coordinating shirt. Very Palm Beach.

A cocaine habit would find him spending hours getting high with the girls as all of the time his request was for a threesome. On one occasion he flew one of my girls to join him with a tall brunette he was dating named Joanne. They stayed at a private secluded beachfront compound in Mexico owned by the then Mexican Government official Melchor Parisquia. The girls phoned me from there in Acapulco and told me all about how it was to be guests in that gorgeous beachfront home that virtually had no other neighbors.

They mentioned his intense cocaine habit and said that he never actually had sex with them. Apparently, he would get as high as he could while watching the two girls having sex together, while playing "director" in their sexual scenario. It seemed he never did bring himself to completion. I never questioned him about any of this either.

To each his own…

After a few years as my client he began to ask me about providing him a girl for a particular fetish he had. His request was to urinate on a girl. He offered to pay any price for that if I could provide him with the right girl. I had several girls who were open to this so I serviced his request. One girl I sent was a gorgeous Afro American gal named Cherie with an unbelievable drop-dead body. Robert was not partial to any particular type and found all women beautiful. During one of our many conversations about it Cherie explained how the scenario went.

"Hi, Cherie. So, how did it go with Robert?" I began.

"Well, Sash, it was a rather interesting experience. First, he placed me in his gorgeous but empty bathtub. He brought out a shower cap for my hair so it wouldn't get wet. He was dressed in his robe a la "Hugh Hefner" and was doing 'cocoa puffs'

Cocoa Puffs is a slang word for cigarettes filled at the tip with cocaine.

"There was another girl there too and she was partying with us but had not joined in yet. He had me get in the empty tub and sit straight up. Then, he began to urinate on me. You know I've done this before so I was totally okay with it. He had the other girl put the shower cap on and join me in the tub and he began to urinate in her mouth! That's one I've never quite seen before. He seemed to get off on it but we never saw him cum. Afterwards, we both showered up, got high for awhile, got paid, and left" she finished.

"Really? I am so confused about why he never ejaculates to completion! "I exclaimed.

"I know. No idea. But I got the $2500 so when would you like to meet to settle up?" she asked.

My cut on $2500 was $1000.

"Whenever is convenient for you today, Sweetie. I'm around all day" I said.

"I have an audition so let me call you back right after I'm through and we'll meet" she offered.

"Sounds good. Speak to you then."

Robert continued phoning me with this request for several years. I always managed to provide him with the right girls to service his needs. Mostly, because they all were actresses who wanted to meet the famous legendary Hollywood producer in the hope of perhaps getting some help from him for their career. There were a few he actually did get nice size acting parts for. Others, he sometimes would help by letting them live in his guesthouse on the property to save them money on the rent. As long as the girls were okay with servicing his request I supposed I was okay with it too. Besides, he had been so generous early on when he agreed to appear in my little three-minute trailer for my film "The Making of a Billboard on Sunset" that I just couldn't say no.

Then things began to change. Robert had left a message that he was interested in something else and requested I return his call as soon as possible.

"Hi, Baby" he said in his handsome deep voice.

He always called me Baby.

"Hi, Robert" I answered.

Even though people who really knew him well called him Bob, I was always partial to full names and preferred calling him Robert.

"I have something different I'd like today, Baby" he began.

"Yes, what might that be?" I wondered curiously.

"I want you to send me a tall, beautiful blonde who will let me shit on her!" he suggested calmly.

"What? Do you mean as in defecate or do you mean as in treat them like shit?" I asked.

Neither option sounded very good but I was actually hoping he meant the latter.

"No, Baby. I mean I want you to send me someone who will let me shit on her, or will take a shit on me!" he said.

I could not believe what I was hearing and at this moment my image of the legendary Hollywood producer I had thought so much of for years was shattered. I had to pause a moment before even responding.

"Robert, are you certain this is what you want?" I asked hoping this might be a joke.

"Yes, Baby. That's what I want" he confirmed.

There were few lines that were drawn or boundaries that existed in servicing the rich and famous. I refused to service anyone interested in any sort of actual physical abuse on the girls, and discouraged aggressive behavior of any kind. I remembered a client whom I had completely refused to service named "Neal" who paid $25,000 to lay bruises on girls over a three-day period. I did not mind servicing a man who wanted a gal to abuse him, however.

"Robert, I can't do this" I said.

"Why, Baby?" he asked surprised.

"I don't have any gals that are willing to do this. The showers are ok, or anything else you might want; but, not this."

Showers, was the slang term for urinating on someone commonly referred to as Golden Showers. Defecating is commonly referred to as Brown Showers.

The truth was I probably could have accommodated his request and found a tall, blonde willing to defecate on him. But I guess this was where I drew my line. Frankly, I simply didn't want to.

"Are you sure, Baby? I spoke with that Heidi Fleiss and she's willing to do it. But I thought I'd ask you first" he said.

"Then call her" I answered.

As far as I was concerned she could have him.

"Okay, Baby. I will" he said.

That would be the last time Robert Evans and I ever spoke. Just like that.

But at least this way, I would still have my fond memories of this legendary man.

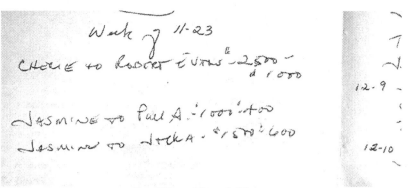

Work of 11-23

Chloe to Robert Evans "2500 —
— 1000

Jasmine to Paul A. :1000 :400
Jasmine to Jack A. — 1500 600

12.9 —

12-10

THE "BLACK BOOK" #1
ROBERT EVANS

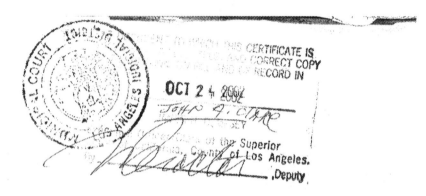

OFFICIAL COURT SEAL of AUTHENTICITY

Chapter 23: Don Simpson's "Top Gun" (with Barry Levinson)

I was quite familiar with the name Don Simpson when he first contacted me and was well aware that he had produced huge mega hit movies like Top Gun with his partner Jerry Bruckheimer. What I did not know however, was how very unusual Don's sexual preferences would be. In the beginning, Don would be the only other client in the history of my thirteen-year reign as the Hollywood Super Madam whom I would offer to run a tab for. I allowed Don to run up a bill for up to $5000 before demanding payment in full. His bills were always paid on time and he showed his appreciation for that by sending me lovely flowers and a thank you note showing that at least he had some class. Unlike my other client, Jon Peters, who had actually showed his appreciation by trying to rip me off on the money. Don was quite the character though. I remember how startled I was during one of our earlier conversations.

"Hey, Don. It's Sash returning your call. What's up?"

We spoke frequently on a rather informal basis.

"Hi, Sasha. How's biz?" he asked.

In those days business was actually very competitive with up to ten other Madams and escort services operating at full force in the Los Angeles area. Don had indicated from time to time in a slightly obnoxious way that he was also using the services of Heidi Fleiss. She had now been on her own a year after first coming to seek employment with me. He would sometimes mention during a conversation that if the girl I sent wasn't a "10" he'd call Heidi. As I was the only Madam who had most of the well known adult film stars and Playboy Playmates, Penthouse Pets, and beauty pageant winners due to my background in casting for films and television, I felt there was no competition and generally laughed it off. Especially since Don was always pleased with anyone he met through me.

"Biz is good, Don. How about you? Working on another terrific project? Or is this one in your bedroom!" I teased.

"Always ends up there, Sash."

We both laughed.

We started chatting about the usual Hollywood gossip and he began to tell me of an interesting story about a wild night he'd recently had followed by an outlandish request.

"Yeah, what a night I had here the other night!" he began.

"Really? You wild?" I teased.

"I had Heidi here. Gave her a ton of Quaaludes and $10,000 to fuck my German Shepherd!" he said.

"No, way!" I exclaimed.

To say that I was shocked was putting things mildly. It was no secret that she had been working as an escort. It was also no secret that she had been using a lot of drugs as evidenced in her emaciated appearance when we first met. Her boyfriend Ivan phoned me several times a week to complain to me about his Sado/ Masochistic relationship with her. It seemed like they were always fighting but somehow maintained some sort of a relationship.

"What are you telling me, Don? That you paid Heidi $10,000 to fuck your dog?"

I was hoping he was kidding. Not because I was all that

174

surprised about Heidi because I wasn't. But as a huge animal lover I found that idea repugnant and unacceptable.

"That's exactly what I'm telling you" he said.

I could not believe my ears! Now what?

"Don, I don't know what to say"

And I really didn't. Moments like these made it hard to keep my personal feelings to myself even though that was one of the more important aspects inherent in being a Hollywood Super Madam. I was even less prepared for what followed.

"You think you have anyone that will do that for me?" Don asked.

I was trying to keep my composure.

"No, Don. I'm sorry I don't" I confirmed.

There was no point elaborating on this as it was likely a moot point.

After all, do stupid people know they're stupid? I was well aware that no lecture I could possibly give would result in some epiphany to Don of how disgusting this was.

"Gee, that's too bad, Sash."

I made up some excuse and got off the phone.

The following day I had a conversation with Ivan who also seemed to know about this incident.

"Ivan, Hi, it's Sash" I began.

"Hello, Sweetheart" he said in his thick European accent. "What's going on?"

We were still great friends until that fateful day I would witness him give up Heidi to the cops.

"Ivan, I was talking to Don yesterday and he told me a most amazing story about Heidi. I was curious if it was true."

"Really? What did he say?"

I chatted with him all the time comparing Hollywood gossip stories.

"He said that he paid Heidi $10,000 to have sex with his dog" I said.

Ivan remained unusually calm.

"It's true, Sash" he confirmed.

"Oh, my! Ivan. You're so calm about it!"

"What can I say, Sash? You know how crazy she is."

So, that was it. Heidi's boyfriend, Ivan, had confirmed that Don had paid her to fuck his dog. Now, I was sure I'd heard everything.

"He said he had to give her an awful lot of Quaaludes to do it" I continued.

"Yeah, that sounds right" he laughed.

We chatted a bit more and I got back to work.

My business with Don seemed to grow until a series of incidents made it impossible to continue. I didn't want to lose him as a client especially since sometimes he'd include his famous director friends who came over to participate in indulging with the girls.

"I'm having my buddy Barry Levinson over tonight so we'll need two" he said.

I was well aware that his film Bugsy with Warren Beatty had just opened.

"What type does he like?" I asked.

"Young and hot with big tits" Don said.

"Got it... a beautiful 5' 8" Dutch model, 24yrs., named Debra. He'll love her."

"Who 'ya got for me?" he asked.

"Venice, a petite gorgeous 22 yr old, busty brunette. Big full natural lips, too."

"Okay. Have them here at my place at 10pm tonight."

"You got it, Don" I said.

I received a disturbing call from Venice the following day.

"Sash, it's Ven. Call me."

She sounded alarmed.

"Hi, Ven. It's Sash. You okay? You sound a little upset" I began.

"Well, I have the oddest feeling. You know I went to see Don Simpson last night. For some reason I have absolutely no recollection of what happened. But I feel like something happened to me" she said.

I found this most concerning especially after the information Don had recently revealed about his fetish for bestiality.

"What do you mean, sweetie? What do you think happened to you? Are you hurt anywhere?" I asked.

I was trying not to sound too alarmed.

"No, I don't feel like I'm hurt anywhere. Just weird. I can't really explain it but I don't think I'll see Don again" she said.

"No, problem, Honey. You know you never have to do anything you don't want to with me."

And it was true. I always made it clear to the girls that my policy was "If there's anything you don't want to do, don't do it." And during my trial all the girls who testified against me confirmed this.

Along with the fact that I had never approached them to work for my service, but rather they had approached me.

"Are you sure you're okay? Would you like me to send you to one of my doctors to be sure?" I offered.

"Thanks, Sash. That's not necessary. I'll be fine. Let me know when you want to meet to settle up."

As I had a tab with Don it was now I who was paying the girls until the tab got to $5000 and then Don paid up on all balances. I owed her a $600 cut from the $1000 she'd earned from the night before.

"Whatever's good for you, Honey. I'm around all day."

Venice and I made a plan to meet later. However, our conversation had left me with an uneasy feeling.

Then a particular incident forced me to completely sever my

business relationship with Don Simpson. It happened shortly after the uneasy meeting with Venice. Don had phoned me to request meeting a pretty young blonde for Saturday night. Was the Pope Catholic? I had hundreds of pretty young blondes for Don to choose from so there was no problem there. Still concerned, I decided to try to get to the bottom of all this and see what the next girl would have to say. After setting up the date with a pretty blonde named Shauna, I went on with business for the day.

I received a disturbing call from her later the following day.

"Really weird Sash. I think Don slipped something in my drink!" she said.

And then it all began to make sense. That was it! As I had absolutely no history of drug use I was basically drug illiterate. I had no idea what he could have slipped them but the theory began to seem painfully clear.

"What do you think he slipped you?" I asked.

The girls always knew far more about drugs than I.

"I have a feeling it was G" she said.

I remembered reading about GHB referred to as the "date rape drug". It had no color and regardless of it's salty taste, could easily be slipped into a girl's drink without her knowing it. This would cause her to fall into a deep sleep for hours and awaken remembering nothing. I was sure she was right.

"I can't be sure, Sash, but I'm definitely not interested in seeing Don ever again" she said.

"Okay, Sweetie. You don't need to. Are you okay?" I asked concerned.

"Yeah, I guess so" she said.

After speaking a bit more we hung up the phone. I decided it was probably futile to debate this with Don. With all his money he likely had great lawyers, too. Plus I had no real proof. I requested that he settle up his tab with me. I said nothing more about it but decided to stay clear of Don Simpson.

-16 Debra To Barry Levinson/Don Simpson
1 000 - 400
17 C_____ __ ____ __

THE DOCUMENT TO WHICH THIS CERTIFICATE IS ATTACHED IS A FULL, TRUE, AND CORRECT COPY OF THE ORIGINAL ON FILE AND OF RECORD IN MY OFFICE.

ATTEST OCT 2 4 2002

JAMES H. DEMPSEY

JOHN A. CLARKE

Executive Officer/Clerk of the Superior Court of California, County of Los Angeles.

By _____ ,Deputy

OFFICIAL COURT SEAL OF AUTHENTICITY

Chapter 24: Roland Joffee's "Scarlet Letter"

· · · · · · · · · · · · · · · · · · · ·

Roland Joffee was the acclaimed director of films like The Scarlet Letter with Demi Moore and Gary Oldman. What few know, however, was that he was one of my earliest clients back in the early 90's. I received the call from a well-known Madam in NY whom I had done some business with named Jackie. This was a common practice between Madams in other cities. Although, since I had offices in 16 states it was generally they who phoned me for the girls, not the other way around. But as long as the client was nice and treated the girls well I never refused the business.

"Hi, Jackie. How's business?" I began.

"Great, Sasha. I'm phoning because I have a VIP client heading to Los Angeles tomorrow and he would like one of your beautiful California girls" she said.

"No problem. Who's the VIP client?"

"Roland Joffee the director"

"Aaahh, yes, I'm a huge fan of his. When is he heading my way?" I asked.

"Tomorrow" she said.

"Sounds good. How much does he usually pay?" I inquired.

"He's quite elegant and likes to take the girl out for a lovely dinner. Doesn't spend more than an hour alone with her in the room afterwards" Jackie instructed.

"I see. Do you charge him just for the hour of intimacy? Or do you include more for the time spent on dinner?"

Jackie was an older Madam who'd been in the business in New York a long time. She was a bit on the hard side and insisted on sometimes charging clients for the time spent during dinner, as well as the private time spent afterwards. Her attitude was "time is money" and she made that clear. I felt that as long as the client was taking the girl out to a lavish meal which included private time afterwards, that I would not charge him for the dinner. But I must admit she had a point.

"I charge him $2000 for two hours including dinner. Plus remember, I take 50%" she said.

That was another difference since I only took a 40% cut from the girls.

"I understand. So, I'll charge him $2000 and we'll split the $1000 cut?" I asked.

"Yes" she answered.

"That's fine, Jackie. Have Roland call me and if you can, let him have a look at my site in case there's someone in particular he likes. Anything I need to know about him?" I asked.

"No, he's pretty basic. Just likes to have a good time" she finished.

"Alright then, Jack. Talk to you later."

The next morning I received the call on my pager. An elegant voice said;

"Hello. This is Roland Joffee calling. I was referred by Jackie in New York."

I returned his call immediately.

"Hi, Roland. This is Sasha. Jackie mentioned you'd be calling. You're interested in someone for this evening?" I began.

"Yes. I had a look at your site and I am particularly keen on the blonde in # 4" he said.

"Oh, yes. She's a beauty. That's Lisa. 22 yrs., a natural 36B, about 5' 8". A real sweetheart too" I said.

"Good, because I don't care for them too busty. I like them thin" he confirmed.

Clients could be terribly specific about what they liked.

"I understand. She's well proportioned. Where will you be staying Roland?"

"I'm at the Regent Beverly Wilshire Hotel in Beverly Hills."

Located across the street from the famous Rodeo Drive, it was a popular choice for celebrities.

"Good choice! You're right across the street from Tiffanys!" I teased.

"Yes. We'll be dining downstairs in the hotel first" he said.

He didn't seem to have a good sense of humor.

"Sounds good. Jackie generally charges you $2000 for two hours including dinner, is that correct?"

"Yes."

"Alright, then. I'll have Lisa meet you in the restaurant. What time would you like her there?" I asked.

"8pm please. And make sure she's dressed well for dinner so I'm not embarrassed" he said.

"Of course. Is there anything else I should know?" I inquired.

Even though Jackie had briefed me it was still my job to be thorough with the right questions.

"Like what?" he asked.

"Like, anything you may want to tell me about? Like what you desire? Another girl to join the two of you or any toys she should bring?"

"No, Sash. Thank you. Just a beautiful girl to take to dinner."

He sounded quite emphatic and terribly straight. Very, English. I loved his accent. Truth was I was a huge fan of his.

Roland was quite a handsome man; dark haired with a bit of a goatee and had directed many wonderful films such as The Killing Fields. The Scarlet Letter with Demi Moore and Gary Oldman was my favorite. I was thrilled just to be speaking with him. As far as I was concerned, whatever he wanted was just fine with me.

"Fine, Roland. As you like. I will have someone simply beautiful to meet you at 8pm in the restaurant. Have a lovely time" I said as we hung up the phone.

The gal I sent had apparently met with Roland's approval for shortly after I received a lovely note from him thanking me for providing him with a lovely evening…

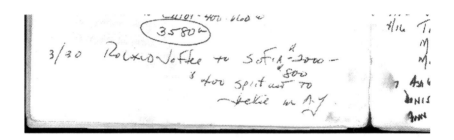

THE "BLACK BOOK" #1
ROLAND JOFFEE
OFFICIAL COURT SEAL OF AUTHENTICITY

Chapter 25: Steve Roth: Not a "Last Action Hero"

Back in the early 90's I was at the peak of my business which seemed to include a 'who's who' of famous producers and directors that seemed to flock to me. One of them was Steve Roth, the producer of "Last Action Hero" starring Arnold Schwarzeneggar. Steve was a sweet guy but, like other famous Hollywood producers he was a bit cheap and believed that beautiful girls should just drop whatever they were doing and rush over to meet him. Granted, he lived in a lovely big home in the flats of Beverly Hills on a street known as Roxbury Drive. But it was like pulling teeth to do business with him. Plus, he always wanted to pay by check.

"Steve, why would a well known producer like you want to pay by check? Can't you get your hands on some cash? I really don't think it's a good idea" I would say.

"Oh, Sash. C'mon, I really don't feel like running out to the bank to get some cash. Can't you just send the girl over?"

He was such a whiner.

"Steve, I can do it once in awhile but I'm really uncomfortable about it."

"Why? My checks are good!"

"That's not the point!. I'm really uncomfortable doing business in anything but cash" I answered firmly.

"Can't you just send over a tall one with big tits? I'll give her $500" he would offer.

"$500?! Steve, you know my prices are $1000 for the hour! As it is I always let the girl stay longer without charging you!" I said.

"Sash, you should be nice to me. My family contributes yearly to the District Attorney's campaign."

And he was absolutely right. His family did contribute to the District Attorney's campaign in Los Angeles, as I would come to know years later during my trial. In fact, this would be one of the reasons my attorney would try to make a motion for a 'change of venue', only to be denied. Steve's name in my infamous Black Book would be one of the ones the judge would place under seal to protect it from public scrutiny.

But for now, he was just trying to bargain me down on my prices.

"Quite frankly, Steve, you're the one who should be careful. You're in my Black Book and you never know..."

I was not one to back down from a threat.

"Okay, Sash. You win. How much?" he asked.

"The usual. $1000 and I'll let you keep her for an extra half hour. Cash" I said.

"Done. Who ya' got?" he asked.

"A real pretty actress about 5' 9", 38D, brunette. Just like you like 'em."

"Sounds fine. Can she come now?"

"Steve! It's 10am in the morning on Saturday!"

"I know, but I'm really horny" he said.

"Okay, let me see what I can do. I'll phone you back."

I phoned Jeanette, the beautiful tall brunette. She was home.

"Jeanette, it's Sasha. Are you up? Tell me, you didn't have too late a night last night?"

"Hi, Sash. No, I stayed in last night. I'm up. What's going on?" she asked.

Jeanette was a really smart gal. She had saved her money and bought her own home at age 32. Also, she was real reliable and didn't do drugs. I was quite fond of her.

"I've got a booking for you. He's a big film director, Steve Roth. His last film was Last Action Hero with Arnold" I said.

You never could be sure where this would lead. Some girls wanted nothing to do with seeing high profile producers while escorting, and some loved it.

"He likes tall, busty brunettes" I said.

"Sounds good. Anything I should know?" she asked.

"Yes. Make sure he pays up front by cash. Not check" I insisted.

"Okay. Should I bring any toys? Am I going to a hotel or to his home?"

"You can bring toys. You're going to his home" I said.

"Cool. When?"

"Now."

"Now? But it's Saturday morning!"

"I understand, but that's what he wants" I instructed.

"Okay then, let me hurry and get off the phone" she finished.

I gave Jeanette the information and she was off. I was a bit surprised when I received her call shortly after.

"Sash, it's me, Jeanette. Call me back. I'm at Steve's house but he gave me a check. I'm not sure what you want me to do" she said on my pager.

I phoned Steve immediately.

"Steven, what's going on? Jeanette says you're paying by check. I thought we settled this already."

I sounded a bit irate at the inconvenience.

"I know, Sash. C'mon, it's no big deal! My checks are good."

"I keep telling you it's not that! I'm just not comfortable about it" I said.

I was really pissed off at the fact that we had come to an agreement on his paying by cash, and now he was violating that. He began to feel like a real pain in the ass.

"Listen, Steven, I don't have time for this nonsense. If you're not going to keep your word, than I'm not going to do business with you" I said firmly.

"Sasha!" he whined.

"I'll do it this one time, but it's the last time, Steven. I mean it. Now put Jeanette on the phone."

"Jeanette, take his check. He's got an hour and a half and not a minute longer" I said.

"Okay, Sash."

Steve was such a spoiled brat who was used to getting his own way. This would be the last time. I didn't need his business and I didn't need his arguing either.

NAME *Sergio (B.H. Hotel)*   NAME *Steve Roth*
STREET   STREET *84 Roxbury*
CITY *(805) 279 6277 (m)*   CITY *(m)(310) 764-1300*
PHONE *(w)(310)281-2924 H (805)290-2574*   PHONE *H 310-274-9133 (m)310-489-0866*
NAME *Seth Warshausky*   NAME *Steve Scott*
STREET *2000 1st Ave. #1404, Sea 98101*   STREET
CITY   CITY
PHONE *(M)206-390-4444 H 206-269-0131*   PHONE *(H)310-278-5551 (c)310-544-1401*
NAME *Steve Jones (310) 264-3357*   NAME *Shazai   B 4: Hotel - R S Katchman*
STREET *10001 Reiesbury*   STREET *10354 Wilshire "33 *506*
CITY *[Bombric 2426 M 90 WritWanda 5]*   CITY *8 760 Shoreham   360-9576*
PHONE *H 310-274-4020 (m) 310-480-5290*   PHONE *310-274-7030 (310)360-6631*
NAME *Steve (D.)*   NAME *Steve Madden   Long Island*
STREET   STREET *52-16 Barnett Rd. Cy 11104*
CITY   CITY *H (914) 254-9835*
PHONE *(m) 310-614-2546 P 577-0226*   PHONE *718-446-1800 (800) 747-6233*
NAME *Maeve Singer*   NAME *Sonny [Business Bath]*
STREET   STREET
CITY *(w)212-643-6633 (b)212-695-2504*   CITY
PHONE *(M)917-861-8466 (b)212-306-1231*   PHONE *(310)273-6618 PM2*
NAME *Stephen (Bath)*   NAME *Sam (AA) Klutznk*
STREET   STREET
CITY   CITY *30 W. 63 St. #15H*
PHONE *(c)310-319-1704 (m) 891-0033*   PHONE *(212) 956-4480*
NAME *Simp Carson (w) 891-0033*   NAME *Sidney Schlenker*
STREET *(m)(805)281-4188 (H)(888)991-8022*   STREET *(H)610 761-9492*
CITY *Hawaii (805) 899-5786*   CITY *(H) 786-2636*
PHONE *310-275-0624 (w)310-842-7800*   PHONE *(310) 278-514*

THE "BLACK BOOK" # 2
STEVE ROTH
OFFICIAL COURT SEAL OF AUTHENTICITY

PART FIVE
"The Conclusion"

Chapter 26: Becoming My Secretary Sherry

By now, my escort empire was at its peak as I got more involved with casting projects for Playboy, Penthouse, and some of the adult films. It was good for my service to employ these title girls since once a gal was featured in a major magazine she could pretty much command her own price. If she was getting a $1000 before, once her layout hit the newsstands she could garner up to $10,000 per introduction from the right client. And I had the right clients. I spent many years acquiring a certain kind of clientele. There were several clients I met along the way whom I refused if I felt they were a problem for the girl, or a problem with the money.

Girls began phoning and writing to me from all over the world. The Prosecuting Attorney would use a box taken from my home as one of the 127 exhibits against me used at my trial. This one box was actually for gals I hadn't employed, but it's contents held over 500 photos and letters from models requesting employment with my service.

I was also in the studio all the time while running to the phone to book the calls to pay for the studio costs which were always over budget. After several record deals that came and went I had finally found what I considered to be my music mentor. He was a high profile record industry guy named Joe Isgro, and known to be one of the best promoters. Joe and I had been introduced through mutual friends and he had signed me to a deal with his current record label Private Eye. He had some brushes with the law in the past as covered in Rolling Stones magazine for alleged payoffs of some kind in the record business. I didn't really know much about it and preferred to stay clear and just concentrate on his deal with me. Joe was a very charismatic dark haired, Italian guy. He had a great ear for music and we clicked creatively almost immediately. I found him to be terribly handsome and definitely my type. My first visit to him reminded of something right out of The Godfather. His office was sat behind big huge gates on a palatial estate with nothing but Ferraris and Mercedes' in the driveway. One had to walk clear across the huge and lavish grounds just to get to where his office was hiding way in the back.

He seemed to like everything I did and we became very close. I never confided to him about my double life however, which would prove to be quite a shock when he saw me later all over the 6 0'clock news. It would be a difficult choice to keep things on a business level since he really turned me on. He was a very intense guy. But alas, I also realized that sex always had a way of screwing up a good friendship. And since I really knew nothing about his personal life, I had no idea whether he was boyfriend material. I used my head instead of my heart and kept things on a business level. We were planning my European tour and the release of my first CD "Right On Track".

Back in my service it had become a tedious task to interview the girls. Calls from new girls were coming in daily and I began to lose my voice. I would always meet each new gal in person and chat with her for up to an hour at a time. Clearly, it was not a good time to lose my voice with all the recording I had at stake. This led to the birth of my Agency Rules; a simple two-page outline that covered most of the do's and don'ts. I found this to be a big help in conserving my voice as it answered many of the questions new girls might ask. I found that offering it to them in the beginning of our meeting helped 'cut to the chase. If a gal didn't get it after that, she probably wasn't smart enough to be employed with my service anyway.

But even with the help of the Agency Rules I really needed a secretary. But whom could I trust?

I was running an illegal escort empire and handling huge amounts of cash. I needed assistance in pre screening the girls since only a percentage of all the photos and letters were really the right type for my now very spoiled clients. Just because a gal was pretty did not guarantee her employment with me. A bad attitude or a drug problem would cause me to end the meeting early. I preferred girls who were sweet and easy to get along with. After giving it some thought, I realized that the only person I could trust was- me. So, once again as it had been so often in my life, necessity became the mother of invention.

Adding on yet another personality into the mix I became my secretary Sherry.

Another reason was that I knew that whoever worked the phones could also walk away with my business. And whom could I really feel safe with in assisting me at running an illegal business anyway? Who could I be sure would not make a stupid mistake and cost me my freedom? I always had to be aware of being "set up" on the phone by some overzealous undercover cop looking to trap me into answering unwanted questions. Posing as my secretary Sherry also provided me a unique opportunity to speak with gals on the phone as someone else. Thereby giving me a chance to really interview them as they were, rather than whom they might try to impress me with once they knew they were chatting with "the boss". It was important that I determine the true disposition of a gal and how she might naturally be with a client to avoid a potential problem with an otherwise somewhat moody or bitchy girl. This could ultimately cost me a valuable client. I explained to the girls that as Sherry, I was strictly talking to them on the phone and that once Sasha approved the potential meeting, we would not be chatting again. So Sherry never had to meet the girls. But I also noticed early on in doing this that people never matched the voice on the phone to the face once we met. Possibly because people had their own idea of what they think someone might look like based on their voice on the phone. I guess I looked different as Sasha than how my secretary Sherry sounded.

Posing as my secretary had many advantages and it worked out incredibly well. I tried changing my voice a bit as I jumped from one personality to the other, and began using it to pre screen all the girls phoning in for appointments. I informed them that as I was in charge of pre screen only, once approval for the meeting to be with Sasha was scheduled, there would no longer be any need for them to meet or speak with Sherry again. Obviously, avoiding any future snafus which might arise as a result of the cross-referencing. I also found that speaking to the gals as the secretary enabled me to get a handle on a girl's true attitude. As opposed to whatever best behavior they might be on while speaking to the boss, Sasha. This made it easier and faster to decide whether or not to move forward with a scheduled interview with Sasha.

It would prove to be an embarrassing moment years later during my trial, when I would receive a count of conspiracy; as conspiracy requires three people. The three people required being: the undercover officer who investigated Sasha, my secretary Sherry, and me. With a packed media room of full of photographers The proud peacock Prosecuting Attorney played the voice tapes that the undercover officer had worn while being wired during her meetings with me. She posed as a girl seeking employment with my service. They must have looked far and wide for just the right girl because she was pretty hot looking. Once the tapes were actually played though, the Prosecuting Attorney would come to realize that the voices of Sherry and Sasha seemed a bit too similar. Prompting my attorney to reveal what we already knew which was; that all along Sherry and Sasha were the same person.

This forced the prosecution to drop the added count of conspiracy because as my attorney put it "One cannot conspire against oneself". This victory however, would be short lived during my trial.

I was now wearing many different hats with at least four different personalities which were essential in running my ever increasing and demanding life. There was: Sasha, the Super Madam; Sherry, her secretary; Babydol, the recording artist; and Jody, the mastermind behind the whole operation.

And at home I was now up to 50 animals...

Chapter 27: The Sting That Stung

My 50 animals had by now become an animal shelter as I couldn't say no to a lost or struggling animal. The menagerie included 35 dogs, 20 cats, ducks (they're messy, but ya' gotta love 'em), rabbits, and the love of my life my miniature potbelly pig "Boo". Animal control had harassed me so many times about the size of my menagerie, that it forced me to pick up and move on several occasions rather than comply with their demand to give them the animals. Relocating from a large home, to an even larger home had now become a way of life. They all needed my love and attention. So, every time I returned home I would go outside and sit and kiss each one so they knew I cared. That's what you do with animals.

Moving also helped keep law enforcement on their toes. My detective lover and I had come to the realization that living together with all my needs wasn't likely. We had grown apart romantically however, he remained fiercely loyal to me. This included 'tipping me off whenever he heard my Sasha name come up in the police department.

"I heard your name come up again. It's going around downtown. You better quiet things down a bit" he warned me.

I did my best to keep a low profile and keep things quiet but it wasn't easy. Apparently, I had become a rather large target over the last few years after the arrest of Heidi Fleiss.

At the time of her arrest there were actually up to 10 escort services operative in the Los Angeles area. I had been told that after she gave up all their names including mine, many were arrested but just didn't make the papers. I remained the only escort service left for quite a few years which made it increasingly difficult to conceal even with all my covert efforts. There would be up to five major police investigations I would manage to slip through before my arrest. My escort empire had grown to include over 300 girls and over a 1000 clients. Even with all the many buffers I had created to insure my safety word just got around in an underground sort of way.

It was now 1997 and I had been operative for 10 years. I had been in and out of several record deals. Life still included choosing songs for my new album, meetings with Joe at the label, planning my soon to be European tour, and of course running my service with the girls to continue making the money to pump into my recording career. I had opted for a Press & Distribution deal with Joe in lieu of accepting an advance. This meant that all he had to do was press the record and get it on the radio and in the stores. Which made it a lower risk for him. I basically turned in a finished product at my expense but would own 70%. This would result in greater profits for me if the record flew. Always the entrepreneurial one, I took more of a business risk as the investor but was passionate and confident about what I was doing. Especially with a promoter like Joe who believed in me.

The need for financial support for my recording project was greater than ever before as we got closer and closer. I was sure it would cost big bucks to promote even with an ace like Joe. This meant that I had to work harder in my escort service than ever before.

A successful escort service depends on the turnover of new girls since clients rarely see the same gal more than once or twice. You needed a lot of high paying clients to hold on to the hot girls. Hot girls go where the money is and if you can't keep them happy, they move on. I certainly had enough clients to keep the girls happy but it was a constant grind. Contrary to what people think, since things are never what they seem, one of the many misconceptions was that all I did was sit around and wait for the phone to ring. Wrong! It's not about sitting at a desk reading a magazine and answering the phone! It's about drumming up business, making appointments, creating bookings, getting people excited about that new girl, making things happen. It was work.

If it were that easy, everybody would be doing it.

And so, this is how it was; working at the studio on the album, running my escort empire, managing the animals at home, being Babydol, Sasha, Sherry, and Jody, and always keeping one step ahead of the watchful eye of law enforcement. Over the last few years I had developed a close relationship with some friends who were bounty hunters. They helped keep me informed as they had their hands in law enforcement as well. We would meet a few times a month for sushi at this great little place in the valley.

"I feel like my phones are tapped. Could you do a wash?" I asked my friend.

A wash was when they went through your home looking for wiretaps. These guys were cool.

"Want to know one way to tell if you're phones are tapped?" he offered.

"Yes. Please tell me."

"Stop paying your phone bill. That's their lifeline between you and the outside world, so if they're watching you, the phone company will know about it and they will not shut your phone off" he said.

"Wow! That's fascinating!" I answered gratefully.

I was sure that it had been no accident that I had met these guys. I needed them in my life.

So, I took their advice and stopped paying my bill. After six months, my fears were confirmed, as the phone was still operative. I had accrued quite a large bill. This was a red flag. Red flag # 2 would rear it's ugly head soon enough.

I had a new boyfriend too, I'd met through my bounty hunter boys, named Craig. He was a cute blue-collar type with muscles and long hair; we fell for each other immediately. We shared the same passion for cars. I was one of the few chicks who knew the difference between a Saleen S7 and a Lamborghini, Gallardo and that impressed him. Amongst the six cars I owned, five were classics I was restoring; a '57 Chevy, a purple '46 Dodge, a' 55 Ford, a '60's truck, and what would become the "Babydol-mobile", my '58 lipstick red Plymouth convertible. It was the size of a living room! So large that my feet barely made it to the pedals! My boyfriend Craig knew about my life from my bounty hunter boys who were always there to protect me. Craig wanted to protect me too.

"Why don't I move you out to my place on the Colorado River? It's on a lagoon and it'll be really hard for the cops to find you out there. There are no street signs, and it's in farm country in a remote location on the Arizona border" he offered one morning over coffee.

"What? I doubt it's big enough, babe. With all my clothes (I needed a house just for that!) my six cars, all my animals, you just don't have enough room for me."

"There's a guesthouse on the property. I can turn it into your wardrobe room, and fence in the property to house the animals. We'll make it work. I love you, Jo" he said.

The men in my life always called me Jo. It seemed endearing.

"You would do that for me?" I asked with a tear in my eye.

"Yup" he answered.

And off we went towards Arizona.

I had hired a new gal to work on the ever-changing needs of my California Dreamin' web site which featured the photos of the girls. The need for a constant update of new photos to keep clients informed and entertained was inevitable. Web masters I hired to work on the site never had any idea that this was an escort service. The site represented itself as a modeling agency with no more information other than "models available on request" along with a selection of various office locations throughout the United States and Europe. My 800 number, which led to a trunk line to, my pager listed in another name provided one of the many buffers I used to remain safe. The web masters I hired never seemed suspicious and never asked any questions about it either.

One busy morning, I received a disturbing call from this new web master. Besides what she said, it was how she said it. My instincts on the phone had grown keen over the years. She sounded nervous and upset and gave me some story about having to check herself into the hospital but was not clear about why or what she was suffering from. It all began to sound like an excuse to distance herself from me. She was returning all my data to me while informing me that she would not be available to work on my site any longer.

"I can't tell you why, I just can't work on your web site any longer!" she urged.

After further questioning I got to the real truth. It seemed she had indeed been contacted by law enforcement about the goings on of my site. My decision to keep this information secret from the people that worked on the site would prove to be a good one not only for myself, but for their safety as well. Law enforcement had threatened and put quite a scare into her. They had concocted some story about my agency being illegal because I did not have permits for the models. They had hoped that she knew more than she did and would spill the beans. There was nothing she could offer them no matter what they threatened her with. Clearly, one did not need a permit to offer a web site of models. But she didn't know that. She was just a gal who changed photos on my web site every week. They put such a scare into her there was little I could do to change her mind. She mailed all my data back to me and never spoke to me again.

This also meant that law enforcement had blown their cover by approaching this gal since it clearly tipped me off. Perhaps they realized this. Red flag # 2.

Life became a bit more dangerous once again. I decided to

place a call to my detective lover and inquire about whether he had heard anything more. I suspected my car might have a "bug" in it and wanted to know where in the car it would likely be placed. A bug is a tactic used by law enforcement to trace a car or eavesdrop in on a conversation. I was curious to know how these things worked and he was always there for me. He suggested I look under the seat and under the hood. I never did find it but felt instinctively that something was there always believing that "if you suspect something is- it usually is". I began to watch what I said while in my car. Once again, my suspicions would prove to be correct. For at the time of my arrest, they would practically take my driver door apart to retrieve it. But for now I decided to lay low for a while.

"Fly below the radar" my bounty hunter friends would say.

Convinced that law enforcement was on my heels I checked in with my detective lover sure that he'd heard my Sasha name come up again. It had been a few months since he last tipped me off. We felt it best for me to develop a code name whenever I phoned him at work.

"Hi. It's Annie."

Annie was for anonymous.

"Have you heard anything more? " I asked.

"Nope. Not a word, babe" he said.

This did not add up. Since all the boys in his department knew who I was, I began to wonder if they were just keeping him out of the loop.

Laying low meant doing less business, which meant losing money, clients, and girls. Since I was still financing the costs for my album I needed to keep the 'money machine' running. Besides, I was closer to record success than ever before with a legendary promoter like Joe Isgro behind me. Planning my tour I was certain that soon I would make the transition from Super Madam to Super Pop Star and leave all this behind me. I had to hang in there a little longer. Needing to plan the budget on promotion for my album, clearly this was not a good time for business to be slow.

Then, just in time I received a call from a gal who called herself Candy. Realizing that the timing was perfect to employ a busty new blonde, I decided to have my alter ego secretary Sherry return the call and set up a meeting with her and Sasha. Candy was available immediately and seemed anxious to start working. This was an important factor since I did not employ girls who were the least bit apprehensive about working for my service. The decision had to be entirely their own. Which is why I leaned towards adult film stars and Playmates in lieu of younger college types who might be undecided. It is for this reason that I had eight counts of Pandering dismissed during my trial. Pandering is defined as: trying to indulge someone's weaknesses. A law created to protect the weaker personality from the more persuasive one. I never tried to persuade anyone to do anything, but rather allowed the gals to tell me what their needs were and what they were looking for.

Candy agreed to a meeting with Sasha at the all night coffee shop known as the "usual place" where I met the girls. Located in the San Fernando Valley area, it supplied a low-key environment catering to an older show business crowd. Plus, the hours worked as it was always open which allowed for all those late night meetings with girls to pick up the money. Our scheduled meeting was for midnight. I knew I'd be driving in from Arizona to work a long day in the recording studio. The four-hour drive each way from Arizona to Los Angeles to record and meet girls was just another adjustment I'd come to know. I began to put a lot of mileage on my Benz. After the briefing by Sherry, I spoke with Candy as Sasha, and explained that I would be driving in from a distance so it would be best to wait inside the coffee shop at a table in case I was a few minutes late.

As I had expected, it was 12:30 at night when I pulled into the coffee shop. I was a half hour late and was a bit taken aback at what I saw. Standing there, outside in the dark, was a beautiful, busty blonde waiting in the parking lot by herself. My instincts sensed immediately that something was wrong with this picture. Why would a beautiful blonde be standing alone, outside at night, especially when I had been clear about waiting for me at a table inside? Caught between the uncertainty of moving forward with this meeting and the need for a new gal during a slow time, I made the conscious choice to move forward but just let her do all the talking. I decided to refrain from discussing anything to do with sex. If she inquired whether the dates included it, I would simply avoid the answer and wink at her. If she were not a cop, than she would understand. If she were, than likely she would pursue more questioning in order to get me on tape discussing sex in the event that she was "wired". Wired meant she was wearing a hidden tape device to record our conversation.

A discussion of a date or an escort is not illegal as long as there is no exchange of money where sex is involved. A girl can get paid to go out on a date and receive compensation for her time and that by itself is legal. The moment sex gets mixed in with money, it becomes illegal.

This all happened within a minute of quick thinking.

I parked my car and approached the gal standing alone outside.

"Hi, are you Candy?" I asked.

Yes. Sasha?" she answered.

"Yes. Let's go in and sit down." I suggested.

Immediately I noticed that her body language was unusual. Her walk was quite masculine, with a gait that seemed as if she were accustomed to wearing something around her waist. Mmmm, like that utility belt with all the apparatus the cops wear. They carry quite a bit on that belt... i.e.: the baton, pepper spray, handcuffs, and it does affect the way they walk. We sat down at a booth. Several things occurred to me with a closer look. She was a real pretty, busty blonde, perhaps a 38D, about 5' 7", pretty shoulder length hair. However, she did not appear to be a gal that made money with her looks. The nails were poorly manicured, and she wore a big dowdy down parka over a masculine pair of pants. Further, she didn't seem like the sort of gal that spent much time on her looks. I would have bet a $100 that her feet weren't pedicured either. She definitely struck me as a cop.

"So" I began, "How did you locate my web site without the secret password?"

"Well, I had been looking for the Cal Dream Inn and stumbled onto yours by mistake" she said.

Wow! What a good answer! My site was called California Dreamin' and the secret password was Caldreamin so that response really threw me quite an unexpected curve ball.

"I called you because I just broke up with my boyfriend and I need to make some quick cash to move" she said.

"I understand. Well, perhaps I can help."

I decided to play along for now.

"What do you normally do?" I continued.

"I'm a part time hairdresser."

As she began her story I started to ponder the moment a bit more. My first thought was; should I take her upstairs to the ladies room and ask her to strip down to her bra and panties so I could view her figure and check for scars or tattoos? If she were an escort, this idea would not bother her at all and taking off her clothes for me would be no big deal. But if she were a cop wearing a wire, likely she would find an excuse to avoid this.

"So, I could really use the work as soon as possible, Sasha" she finished.

"I see. Do you have any pictures?" I asked.

"'Yes, right here" she said pulling out some very amateur photos.

"I'll need some good professional looking ones since that's what I'll be showing my clients."

A bad photo of even the prettiest girl might cause a rejection.

"If you don't know a good photographer, I can help you with one that will cost very little. Perhaps he can do me a favor and shoot just a few for free" I offered.

Clearly, I was trying to keep her comfortable.

"No, thanks. That's okay. I'll get you the kind you need" she said.

She kept talking while I kept thinking. My mind was working fast taking notes of everything in front of me. This girl was very attractive for a cop, but a bit too masculine to be considered upscale like the kind of girls I worked with. However, she had given me an incredible answer for finding my website! She said that her name was Candy, and she claimed to be a hairdresser who needed money to move right away because of a break up with her boyfriend. All this seemed plausible except for; why she would stand alone waiting outside for me in the dark instead of inside where it was warm and comfortable like most girls would have? Could she be a cop? Was she wired right now recording our conversation? What if I took her upstairs and her reluctance to disrobe led to an altercation? Would 20 police officers come busting in thinking she'd been "made" or found out? I decided it best not to take a chance on that for now. I had to come up with another plan.

"How much do you think I can make? What do you charge for the dates?" she questioned.

"Dinner dates average between $1500-$3000 depending on the time involved" I said.

Out came the Agency Rules, which I handed her. This gave me a chance to look at her and think a moment longer. There was nothing too incriminating on there aside from; 'Bring your own condoms', 'Don't be late', 'Bra & panties should match', etc.

"I might have a job for you for $3000. You would fly to Colorado for dinner" I offered.

My plan was to throw her off guard and not let her see I was suspicious about anything.

"Sounds great! I'm available immediately" she said.

With split second thinking I decided what to do. I'd wrap the meeting up and offer to walk her to her car. Once there, I'd make a note of the license plate and give it to my bounty hunter boys. They could run the plate and tell me whom it was registered to. Perhaps we might be able to trace it to law enforcement. I decided to wrap the meeting up.

"Okay, then. Let's go. I'll walk you to your car" I offered.

We left the coffee shop together and proceeded to walk towards her car. As we passed my Mercedes, I turned my head to glance and make sure my car was okay. Turning my head to the right to see, I snapped it back to the left and she was gone! Just like that! In a split second of taking my eye off her she was gone. It happened that fast. I looked all around for signs of an exit but saw none. She was nowhere in sight and had escaped in an instant into the dark night. Missing my only chance to get an eye on her license plate, I retreated back to my car and got in.

I was stunned at how quickly she was able to disappear.

Driving back to the hotel I'd been staying at while in town, I began to recap the conversation in my mind; fortunately, I had been careful not to say anything too incriminating, nothing had really happened. Could I have been wrong about this girl? Did she think perhaps I was walking away as I turned to look at my car and she just left? Was she there in the dark in the parking lot somewhere walking to her car and I just didn't see her? Maybe she really was just a gal seeking employment. With the costs of my album gnawing at me, I began for the first time in my life to second-guess myself.

Business was slow as I continued to keep a low profile. I was still working in the studio spending money on my tracks which were well over budget as usual. I had not heard a word from Candy; the gal whom I suspected was a cop. That was strange too. If she were a cop, why wouldn't she have moved forward immediately with the dinner date for $1500 in Colorado that I had offered her?

Confident that this album I had worked on with Joe would finally be the vehicle to whisk me away to pop stardom, I began to think about my future. Perhaps I should keep some sort of diary about my life as a madam? After all, I'll be way too busy with touring and recording soon and will probably forget about all these years with my 'double life. All the twists and turns and the investigations I'd been through. But I was never one for keeping thoughts in diaries. I worked alone and always kept everything to myself. Perhaps I could write a short treatment like a synopsis for a movie? So, that's precisely what I did. I wrote a ten-page manuscript briefly outlining my life as a Super Madam, the clients, girls, my 007 alter egos, and my love affair with the detective and how I'd received immunity. Because of my loyalties to those who have been there for me, I vowed never to reveal the true identity of my detective. I was glad that at least I'd have something to reference to since I had a hunch that my life was about to change in a big way.

One evening while relaxing at home with my boyfriend, Craig, I pulled out my ten-page manuscript.

"What's that?" he asked.

"Oh, just some manuscript I wrote about my life as a madam" I said.

"Really? Let me read it?" he asked.

I handed him the manuscript. It didn't take him very long to read it.

"Wow! Babe, you should write a book!" he exclaimed.

"What? Why? This is just a brief summary so I don't forget things since Joe's getting ready with my tour."

"This is fascinating stuff and I think people would really get off reading it!" he said sounding genuinely excited.

"Really? Gee, it doesn't seem all that interesting to me" I said.

"That's because it's your life."

And then, I put my manuscript away and forgot about it for a while. Besides, red flag # 3 was right around the corner.

With the need for a new computer basically, so I could work on the arrangement of photos on my web site, it seemed more cost effective to explore the possibility of Web TV. It had just come out and seemed like a good solution. All one had to do to get online service was hook it up to a television and the online image would appear on your TV screen. All you needed was a phone line.

It was fast, cheap, and seemed easy to install. So we drove to the local department store to purchase one.

After bringing it home we began to have some difficulty with installing it. No matter how hard we tried it wouldn't turn on. Craig spent several days working on it.

"Let's just call an electrician. They won't charge too much to just come and install it" he suggested.

So I found an electrician in the remote area to come over and locate the problem. He arrived to assess the confusion and seemed to know what the difficulty was.

"Aaah, I see your problem right here. You've got an outside line somewhere else in the house drawing power from an open line. This is making it impossible for the phone to distinguish a disconnect so it can hang up and connect you to your Web TV" he said.

I shot Craig a look as we both knew exactly what this meant.

"Let's just look around and see what we can find" the electrician suggested.

Uh oh, I thought. Do we want to find? I did not want to appear nervous in front of this stranger in my home. We were living in such a remote location that everybody knew everybody, but nobody knew about me. And that's just the way I wanted it. We let him search but he could not come up with anything.

"This just doesn't make sense! I can't find anything but I'm sure there's an open line here somewhere" he confirmed.

Craig and I just stared at each other. It made perfect sense to us. This meant that law enforcement was onto us. Our little hide out existence was ruined. I paid the electrician and sent him on his way. Red flag # 3.

It had been weeks since my last meeting with Candy at the coffee shop and I hadn't heard a word. Now I was convinced I must have been wrong about her being a cop. I remembered clearly what my instincts were that day but why hadn't she grabbed the bait? I had left messages for her regarding the dinner date in Colorado but hadn't heard back. If she was a cop why was she ignoring my calls?

Then suddenly, there was a letter from her waiting at my mailbox. Using a separate location to receive mail away from my home was another buffer I had created to try to insure my safety. I noticed the name Candy on the outside of the envelope and went immediately to my car to sit and open it. She was apologizing for not returning my calls. Apparently, an ill-fated attempt at reconciliation with her boyfriend had caused her delay, but now she had concluded that her relationship with him would never work out. She was ready to get to work and wanted me to understand and not consider her a flake. It had been over month since our last meeting. I decided to give her a call.

"Hi, Sasha. You got my letter?" she asked.

"Yes, I did."

I decided to let her do all the talking.

"Yeah. I went back with my boyfriend but things really didn't work out and I'm sure they never will" she began.

"I understand" I said.

"Anyway, I have this one guy I've been seeing for years on the side. He pays me $1000 per day. I know him for a few years and he wants a girl to party with us" she said.

"Why would you spend all day with someone for $1000 when you can make that with me in one hour!" I questioned.

"I don't know. Maybe because I know him" she answered,

This really made me think. I was familiar with the fact that a conviction of one girl would never be enough to pursue a case against me. They needed a conviction of several girls to put together a decent case. She was only asking for one girl. Could this be legit?

"Have him look at my web site and let me know if there's someone on there he's interested in. He needs to understand that my price is $1000 for one hour, not one day" I said.

I decided to see where this went as I was sure of the law and knew that using just one girl would not be enough to put a successful case together.

"Okay, I will. His name is Robert" she said.

"Fine. Have him call me" I suggested.

A few days later Robert phoned me. He had a thick Middle Eastern accent.

"Hi, Robert. This is Sasha, returning your call."

"Hi, Sasha. Candy has told me so much about you. I've been admiring the beautiful models on your web site" he said.

"Thank you. Anyone in particular you like? Candy mentioned that you're looking to party with another girl so, will it be the three of you?"

"Actually, Sasha,. I did not want to hurt Candy's feelings but I'd rather see a new girl by myself" he said.

This still didn't feel right. But he was only calling me for one girl so it seemed possible he was for real. If it were a set up he'd be requesting at least two or three girls to insure the conviction.

"I see."

I had to think quickly on who to suggest to him. Which girl could I send that I could clue in here? I decided on a beautiful Hawaiian gal named Leanne. She was gorgeous, smart, and I felt secure that I could make her aware of my concerns and that she could handle things. I needed to know if Robert was a cop.

I had done some really nice favors for Leanne so I was confident that she would aid me.

"Have a look at # 11. She's a gorgeous beauty pageant winner from Hawaii named Leanne. I think you'll like her" I suggested.

"She looks perfect, Sasha. Let's do it" he said.

"Fine, Robert. I don't know if Candy explained things to you but my prices are a bit different than what you're probably used to with her. A date with Leanne for one hour would be $1000."

"That's no problem. I'll be staying at the Century Plaza Hotel in Century City. I'd like to have her meet me there tomorrow afternoon. I'll phone you when I check in about an hour before with the room number. Will that be enough notice for her?" he asked.

"Yes, that should be fine, Robert."

With his thick accent I was sure that Robert couldn't possibly be his real name.

"Okay, then. It's all set. I'll phone you tomorrow" he finished.

Yes. Speak with you then" I said.

I took a deep breath before phoning Leanne. I needed her to understand that this was a delicate situation that required her help. I'd known her for a while and was hoping she'd be able to check this out for me. After rehearsing the scenario a bit in my mind I gave her a call.

"Leanne? Hi, it's Sasha."

"Hi, Sash. What's up?" she asked.

"Well, sweetie, I have a situation I need your input on."

"Really? What?" she asked.

"I've got a guy and quite honestly, I need a girl to check him out and see if he's a cop" I began.

"Wow! I see. How do you suggest we do that?"

It sounded as if she might be willing to help me.

"Go to the job and see him. Spend some time talking to him and get him relaxed. Then, have him take his clothes off and fuck him. If he doesn't fuck you, don't ask for any money. Tell him you changed your mind, maybe that you realize this is not for you or something. As long as you don't have sex with him and accept the money, he can't do anything to you. If he fucks you, then he's not a cop and you can accept the $1000" I said.

She pondered my plan in silence for what seemed like a long moment.

"Gee, Sash. That's brilliant!" she exclaimed.

"Thank you"

"This way, nothing can really happen unless there's sex. And, if there's sex than he's not a cop!" she said.

"Precisely"

"You are amazing. How'd you come up with that one?" she asked fascinated.

"Practice my dear, practice" I said.

We chatted a bit more and I began to feel a little better. Glad that I could come up with a plan. I let her know that I'd be phoning tomorrow with the room number and informed her that it would be at the posh Century Plaza Hotel. She agreed to be ready.

The next day Robert phoned as promised.

"Hi, Sasha. It's Robert. Is everything okay?" he asked.

"Yes, Robert. I have Leanne ready and waiting to meet you."

"Fine. Have her come to room 612. I'll expect her at 3pm."

"No problem, Robert Have fun" I said.

It occurred to me at that moment that Candy had still not actually booked a job with me.

"Hi, Leanne, it's Sash. He's there in room 612"

"Got it, Sasha. I'll head over there and call you immediately after" she said.

I would put something real nice together for her assisting me with this. But then, the girls knew I was always there for them too, whenever they needed anything. If they were in a jam, needed a ride to their plastic surgery, or someone to hold their hand during an abortion. I'd been there time and time again. And now, Leanne was helping me. It was going to be a long afternoon as I waited for her call.

Startled by my pager, it was 5pm when I heard from Leanne. Apparently, my stress had taken its toll and before I knew it I had closed my eyes and two hours had whizzed by. I returned her call immediately, anxious to hear the results of what had transpired with Robert.

"Hi, Leanne. It's Sasha. So, what happened? Did you fuck him?"

This was a critical way of determining whether Robert was a cop. If he were, clearly sex would have been prohibited.

"Oh, yeah. What a doll!" she said.

"Really? How big was his dick?"

"Actually, he had a pretty big dick for a little guy!"

"Why? How short was he?"

At 5' 9" Leanne towered over most guys once she put her high heels on.

"Like 5' 5". But he was so sweet, Sash. We talked for about a half an hour first."

"What about?" I asked curiously.

"Oh, he wanted to know all about me."

"Did he ask any questions about me, or our relationship? You know like how much of a cut I take, or anything about the money?" I asked.

"Nope. Not a word. I don't think he's a cop, Sash. I fucked him and he gave me a $1000. I've got your cut" she said.

Right now my 40% cut was the farthest thing from my mind.

"Gee, Leanne. I don't know how to thank you, sweetie. Did he ask for your telephone number?"

"No, Sash. He didn't. Really, he seemed like a pretty cool guy."

"Well, I guess that's that then. We can wait until tomorrow to settle up on my cut. You go have a nice evening now" I finished.

"Okay. Talk to you tomorrow" she said.

I hung up the phone and remained in my chair stunned. My instincts had served me well for many years and never been wrong. But Leanne confirmed that Robert had sex with her so, I guess that meant he wasn't a cop.

Or so I thought...

Dear Sherry,

Hello my name is Candy and I spoke to you about possibly working for the service on Thursday of last week. You gave me and address that I could send some photos to you but unfortunately they aren't ready yet. I'm sorry about that, it makes me so mad.

Anyways, I'm a California blonde, 5-6, 34D-24-34 with pretty blue eyes and a great tan. I don't mean to brag but I can turn a few heads. Oh yeah, I'm 24 years old.

As I told you before, I've worked enough in the past to know how it works, but I'm definitely not worn out or overworked. I am very responsible and professional and very easy to get along with.

Hopefully the delay with my pictures won't delay my interview with you. I am looking forward to meeting with you.

Thanks, Candy

LETTER FROM CANDY, THE COP EXHIBIT #20 FROM COURT RECORDS

Chapter 28: The Arrest

Robert phoned the following day to thank me. He said that he was leaving the country and would phone in a few months when he returned. I still had a haunting feeling...

It was April 1999 and Joe and I were mastering my album over at Capital Records in Hollywood. They had a terrific mastering facility. I was excited about the fall tour we were planning but still felt I needed money to insure the right promotion campaign. I began to think about securing things at home before my departure.

Thoughts began to cross my mind as to what would happen to all my girls that depended on me. Who they would turn to after I was gone? Granted, there was no one left in Los Angeles but me, but perhaps I could figure out an alternate arrangement for them. I contacted other madams I knew in cities like Chicago and New York and made arrangements for them to take my girls. And why wouldn't they? I knew the most gorgeous girls from all over the world.

I had phoned Robert to check in and see if he had returned from his trip but he had not returned my call. I left several messages. It had been a few months since his last booking with Leanne. His long absence with no return call, plus Leanne's admission that she had sex with him got me thinking that maybe I had been wrong about suspecting him to be a cop. There was no word from Candy either.

Three months later I finally heard back from Robert.

"Sasha, it's Robert. I've just returned from my trip and I have great news" he began.

"Hi, Robert. Nice to hear from you again. What's the news?"

"I have just been with the Royal Family in Kuwait. It seems they would like me to fly four of your prettiest girls there to meet them and will likely keep them as guests in the palace for three weeks. Security will be escorting them along with myself, and we will be traveling on the private plane of the Royal Family" he said.

I tried to choose my words carefully so as not to offend him. Except for the Sultan of Brunei it was not my practice to fly girls to that part of the world.

"Thank you, Robert. I appreciate your generous offer however; much needs to be discussed before I would ever considering sending four of my girls to Kuwait. Even as guests of the Royal Family" I said.

"Sasha, I will be personally escorting them. I have been working security for the royal Family for years and they will be very well looked after" he promised.

"Yes, I'm sure. We still really need to discuss this further. This is not a decision I can make in one day. For one thing, I will need to be able to contact them at any time day or night by phone so I will need to be furnished with all private numbers where they will be residing" I began.

"No problem. I will give you my private mobile number as well and you will be able to contact me at any time" he said.

"Also, my girls earn top dollar. I am sure that a trip like this would cost at least $30,000 per week per girl."

"That is also no problem. Money is no object to the Royal Family" he confirmed.

It sure did sound tempting. I instantly did the math in my head and realized that this one job would bring in revenue of $360,000 with a 40% cut of $144,000 coming to me! This was just about what I needed to insure the promotion on my soon to be released album. Convinced that things were falling into place, perhaps this would be my last booking as Sasha. I would pump the promotion money into the album insuring it's successful debut with Joe Isgro behind me. Then, I could walk away from my life as a madam and finally make my transition to pop stardom. Yes, this would be my last job. But there was still much to consider.

"Well, that's good to know but we really need to talk. I have to explore things further before I take the responsibility of placing four girls on a plane to that country" I said.

"I understand completely, Sasha. I am available to answer any questions you might have. I want you to feel completely comfortable and secure with me" he said.

"Thank you, Robert. I'm glad you understand."

"As a matter of fact, why don't we sit down and discuss things. I will be back at the Century Plaza in a few days with a friend of mine. Perhaps you can send over two of the girls you are considering sending so we can see whom you have in mind. We will spend an hour with them first in the room, and then you and I can meet afterwards, downstairs in the restaurant to discuss" he suggested.

It sounded like a reasonable plan except or one thing... this would mean that I would have to break my sacred policy of 'never meeting clients in person'. But with the potential risks of such a trip there would be no other way but to sit and discuss things. There would be no way I would ever have considered a trip such as this without looking straight into the eyes of the gentleman in charge. That was my only true meter. Even with my client the Sultan of Brunei, I insisted on accompanying the girls to London on the first few trips to have a look at their man in charge. And they flew on the Sultan's private plane. But assuming Robert was sincere and all was safe, this meant I could really make the final monies required for my record and walk away! I decided to at least take the meeting to sit and discuss things further.

"Okay, Robert. We'll handle it as you suggest. I'll send two top girls to you and your friend first. They will be the two that I might consider sending on this trip. You'll each be in separate rooms for an hour for $1000 per girl. When you're ready, phone me and I'll meet you afterwards down in the restaurant so we can talk" I instructed.

"Fine, Sasha. I will do as you say. We will be checking into the hotel in two days. We will see the girls at 7:30 pm and you and I can meet at 8:30. I will contact you with the room number when we check in" he said.

"Okay, then. Speak with you then" I said and hung up the phone.

So many thoughts ran through my mind. I needed to be sure that Robert was sincere and that my girls would be treated well and be safe. The idea of four of my gorgeous girls running around in a foreign country like that made me nervous. In all my years of running my escort empire I had always chosen to avoid taking that path. It had not been the first time it had been offered to me.

I just never needed it that much nor was I comfortable about it. But what if Robert was sincere? What if he really had been doing security for the Royal Family? I would have my bounty hunter boys check him out of course. What if all of this was real? Was I really going to walk away from this business I had created from nothing, and turned into a profitable empire? Would I? Could I?

The reality of this was something until now, that I hadn't really given much thought to. This business of mine, illegal as it was, still offered me a sense of security. No matter what ever happened I could always make money. I had the responsibility of my 50 animals to feed in my shelter, as well as supporting myself.

I decided to take the first step and have the meeting so that meant deciding on which two girls for Robert and his friend. My girls Kelly and April came to mind. Kelly was a 5' 11" busty model with long brown hair that framed her gorgeous face. She was real sharp and had always impressed me as the kind of gal that could handle herself in any situation. April was a 5' 9", blonde, California actress type that spoke several languages fluently. She had dual residence in the USA and Canada and was an experienced traveler. I decided they would be a perfect choice for this trip. I refrained from mentioning anything about it to them until I was sure about Robert and his intentions. For now, Kelly and April would just be booked on another $1000 hour job until further notice.

But something still did not feel right. My instincts were blaring. But why? Surely, Robert could not be a cop. After all, he had sex with my girl Leanne and paid her! That was months ago. Further, I had phoned him repeatedly during his absence while he was away and he had not returned my call for some time. But why did I still have this gut feeling?

That night I mentioned to my boyfriend Craig that I was going to make the meeting. He begged me not to go.

"Don't worry, babe. Everything will be alright" I promised.

He had an uneasy feeling too. I began to think about it but put my concerns aside.

Maybe it was just the reality of facing the decision that it might really be my last booking. And the uncertainty of all that it might mean to end my life as a madam. With all the pressure of having a business that included 1000 clients, 300 girls, the years of evading law enforcement with all it's dangers and great risks, the many hats I wore to accomplish things which began as necessitated living a double life; It seemed at the end of the day that even with all of this, the constant flow of money made me feel secure. I made plans to drive into town from Arizona and stay in the hotel. Craig would stay behind and take care of things at home.

Two days later I heard back from Robert as promised. I had contacted Kelly and April and they had confirmed the booking. The plan was set. They would meet Robert and his friend in their two separate rooms, and Robert and I would begin our discussion of the trip afterwards in a restaurant downstairs in the Century Plaza Hotel. The girls and I would settle up my cut later.

I had checked into my hotel earlier that day and was in Los Angeles waiting to see him.

"Sasha, it's Robert. We've just checked in at the hotel in room # 612, and # 614. Will you have the girls ready for 7:30 tonight?" he asked.

"Yes, Robert. No problem" I said.

"Good. There is a coffee shop downstairs for us to meet afterwards at 8:30."

I realized that I had no idea what Robert looked like aside from being short as Leanne had stated.

"I see. How will we find each other? I have no idea what you look like" I said.

"Just ask for me at the front. They'll show you to my table" he suggested.

"Sounds good. I'm sending two of my top girls. A tall, busty brunette named Kelly, and a beautiful blonde named April. I think they'll be perfect for the trip. I haven't mentioned it to them yet until we speak but let me know what you think" I said.

"Will do, Sasha. See you tonight" he said.

That uneasy feeling was gnawing at me again.

It was a warm summer night on June 9, 1999. I had decided to pull out the stops and opted for a stunning crème colored, 2 pc. Chanel skirt suit. Jewelry was on with a pair of diamond stud earrings and bracelet to match, along with my gold and diamond Rolex. I had a glamorous meeting that evening as Babydol, which was to finish an hour before meeting Robert but felt it wouldn't hurt to make a good impression.

I drove into the valet of the Century Plaza at precisely 8: 30. Walking through the empty lobby, I made my way downstairs to the coffee shop. I approached the cashier and requested she show me to Robert's table. She seemed as if she had been expecting me.

"Oh, yes, he's waiting for you right over here" she said as she showed me to his table.

A short little Middle-Eastern man greeted me.

"Sasha, you are so pretty!" Robert sneered.

"Thank you" I answered politely.

"We really enjoyed the two girls you sent. They will be perfect for the trip" he said.

The conversation continued for about a half hour as I made my demands clear. Robert outlined how things would proceed. We discussed the importance of providing ample security for the trip, and providing me with the necessary phone numbers so that the girls would be available to me by phone at any time. I still needed to check him out with my bounty hunter boys before confirming.

"The girls are to be paid up front $30,000 apiece at the start of each week" I instructed.

"No problem, Sasha."

"I prefer they each have their own private guest quarters, away from any other males except those confirmed with security. You can send for them as you like, and they are to be escorted by security whenever they leave their rooms" I insisted.

"No problem" he repeated again.

It seemed like the initial part of our meeting had gotten off to a good start. As Robert continued speaking I began to search the face in front of me. He was indeed, a short little Middle Eastern man with a slight goatee of hair on his face. There was nothing terribly descript about his appearance. He was dressed in an average looking 2-pc suit. Outside of that, there was nothing that would distinguish him in a crowd. His English was very good but with an accent.

"Sasha, my friend who was with me tonight would very much like to meet you" he said.

Clearly, we were getting ready to end our meeting.

"Fine. Bring him in" I suggested.

"Oh, I would but he's embarrassed as he's dressed in his traditional long white Thobe. Perhaps we can go upstairs to meet him on the way out" he said.

There went that uneasy feeling in my gut again. I just wanted to hurry and get out of there.

"Okay, then. Just for a minute. I've got somewhere else to be."

He paid the check and we got up to leave. We walked upstairs and as I set one foot onto the carpet of the lobby I looked up and within seconds I was surrounded by at least twenty cops flashing badges in my face! There was complete mayhem! They were all shouting to me at the same time. They were so excited at my capture I could barely make out what they were saying, but managed to hear words like "arrested for pimping". My worst nightmare was staring me right in the face! I was being arrested in the lobby of the Century Plaza Hotel! Knowing the first golden rule I had always taught the girls in case this ever happened to them "don't say a word", I immediately encased myself in a vacuum of silence. Their lips were moving as I began to hear nothing but the beating of my own heart. Like a television whose picture was on with the sound muted out I was in complete shock. My gut feeling had been right all along.

I had been set up.

They led me downstairs into a hidden room used for interrogation, which looked like the inside of some hi tech submarine. Posters with "Wanted" on them framed the walls. The room was filled with overzealous police officers waiting to question me. They began to go through my handbag searching for evidence. They came upon my portable wizard used to store all my phone numbers of clients and girls.

"We'll just take this" the officer said.

Then Robert approached me.

"Sasha, I have been after you for so long. You were my worthiest opponent. If I were going to do what you did, I would've done it just like you" he snickered.

I stared straight at him but said nothing. His name obviously wasn't Robert as I had suspected. He began to try to trap me into some kind of a confession.

"Look, she's got everything in here! Victoria's Secret, Neiman Marcus."

They all laughed.

"I guess she won't be needing these anymore where she's going" he joked.

They laughed again. It began to seem like a real party.

"You're going to prison for a very long time" Robert said.

"I see. Do I get my phone call now?" I asked.

Realizing they were getting nowhere with me they gave me my one phone call. My bounty hunter boys answered the phone.

"Hi, it's me. I've been arrested. I'm at the Century Plaza Hotel but they're taking me down to the station" I said.

"We know. They've got Craig. They took him all the way to a jail in Arizona instead of one nearby because he wouldn't cooperate. Which one are they taking you to?" my boy asked.

"I think they said Van Nuys" I answered.

I didn't want to ask about Craig or say anything with them sitting there.

"Got it. We'll meet you there" he assured me.

"Okay, Thanks. Bye".

Meanwhile, the officers continued their party.

"We'll really have a press conference about this one!" the officer said.

Press conference? That was something they had after a movie premiere or a big case! What were they talking about? I was confident even then, that this was a minor problem for me. It would require the right attorney and the right favor card. I would find out whom we needed to call and wash all of this mess under the rug and it would be forgotten. I hung up the phone and sat there silent. Then, they led me into the back of a squad car.

Sitting there many more things raced through my mind.

Where had they taken Craig? I knew he would never talk to cops. He was too much of a rebel and too protective of me. He wasn't afraid of cops. My bounty hunter boys would get him out as soon as they were able. But what about all my animals? We had a Rotweiler, a Great Dane, and Shepherds; big dogs that I was sure would be alarmed with all the chaos going on at home. I was praying that they had not hurt the animals. Law enforcement had apparently timed this just right. Craig and I were arrested at exactly the same time to avoid tipping each other off.

And what about my girls Kelly and April? Had they been arrested too? If so, where were they? Did they cooperate and confess to avoid prosecution by turning evidence against me? I needed to find out where they were. As soon as I could I would have my guys check the computer and see if their names came up. If they did not, that would mean that likely they were arrested and had turned on me to receive immunity. Although the girls and I had many discussions about just what to do at a time like this, I remained sympathetic to them and understood their fear. We would have to check and see as the evening progressed. But for now it seemed, I was facing the beginning of my worst nightmare.

I was going to jail...

Chapter 29: Trial

I was taken down to the Van Nuys Police Department finger-printed and booked. Fortunately, my bounty hunter boys were there to bail me out immediately so I never saw a night in jail.

Not that night, anyway...

Upon returning to my hotel I found my room in a complete shambles. My hotel room had been raided too. There had also been the "bug" that had indeed been placed in my car just like I had suspected. And then it hit me; they had taken my "black book" of clients and the ten-page manuscript I had written detailing my life as a Super Madam! Always kept well hidden, I had this one time removed them from their secret hiding place. Robert's alleged offer of a big job to Kuwait required many notes and files on which girls might be appropriate, and I was considering shopping my manuscript as a book deal. Never dreaming this would ever happen I had removed them this one time from their sacred hiding place and now the cops had them! I sat for a moment, shocked at the impact of this disaster. I needed to change hotels immediately so I could feel comfortable enough to think so the Sportsman's Lodge in Studio City seemed like a good choice. Likely, as long as I remained here in the very hotel they had just raided, the odds were my every move was being watched.

It was 6 am and I had not slept yet. After I made bail a search on the computer told me that my girls Kelly and April had probably cooperated and turned evidence against me to avoid prosecution. Their names were nowhere in sight. Surely, if I had been arrested so had they. I tried phoning home to check on things but there was no answer. My bounty hunter boys would return at 10am to take me to a good attorney they felt would be able to help me. I had 8 days left until my arraignment wherein I would hear the charges and the amount of counts held against me. Each count carried it's own designated jail time. The right attorney with some clout would be able to make this all go away.

Or so I thought...

At 10am my boys showed up. On the drive over I phoned Leanne. As of now my horrible night was still a big secret.

"Leanne, it's Sasha" I began.

"Hey, Sash."

She acted as if nothing was wrong. I would soon find out of her arrest later that day for the $1000 booking with Robert that had transpired over two months ago. But for now, things were still calm.

"Listen, I really need to know something" I said.

"What?"

"Are you absolutely sure that you fucked my client Robert and he paid you a $1000?" I asked.

"Absolutely" she confirmed.

I began to ask her the same questions about his specifics like the size of his dick etc., which I had asked about 2 months before and she was giving me the exact same answers. This led me to believe that she was telling the truth since a lie is more difficult to remember.

"Okay then, Honey. Bye" I said.

We arrived at the attorney's posh office in Beverly Hills. Since I was the only one who knew exactly what evidence had been retrieved from my belongings during the police raids, it was up to me to convey all this to him so he could be aware of how serious things looked.

"How much will this cost?" I asked.

"I can handle everything for you for about $5000" he said.

I pulled out the $2500 I had brought with me for a retainer fee and paid him on the spot. We chatted a few minutes more and I left feeling a little bit better that perhaps this attorney could make my little problem go away.

The rest of the day I tried to relax. My boyfriend Craig had been released from the jail he had been taken to in Arizona and was on his way in to meet me. I stopped at the grocery store to pick up a few things for us to have at the hotel. My plan was to have a nice quiet time unwinding in his arms and then fuck our brains out. I returned to the hotel to find Craig waiting there to greet me. He had a disturbing look on his face.

'Babe, I don't know how to tell you this but you're all over the 6 o'clock news!" he said.

"What? What are you talking about? This is no time for jokes. I've had a really rough night."

"I'm not joking! Come in and see for yourself " he answered.

And indeed it was. Not just on the 6 o'clock news either, but the 8, 10, and 11 o'clock and even Jay Leno was cracking jokes about me on the Tonight Show! In fact, it was everywhere. My secret was out. As I watched it on TV I realized that this was the press conference the cops had been talking about. Almost instantly, calls began pouring in from news journalists and television shows from all across the country. The Today Show, Diane Sawyer, Larry King, you name it. They all wanted to speak to the notorious Madam that had just been arrested. My case was making headlines around the world as the tabloid photographers were slipping notes under my hotel door. Apparently, someone in the hotel had tipped them off and they were offering me over $100,000 for an interview.

"Don't speak to anyone!" my attorney instructed.

Everyone knew who I was now and what I was running from so it made no sense to change hotels again. Joe called from my record label. He had seen it on the news as well.

"Are you okay? Do you realize how much trouble you're in?" he asked concerned.

"Don't worry, Joe. I'll get out of it."

"Is this OCID or Vice?" he asked.

OCID stood for Organized Crime Internal Division and was taken much more seriously than an ordinary Vice case.

"OCID. Why? We can still put my record out, can't we?"

Joe remained silent ignoring my question.

"Do you need anything? Do you have a good attorney?" he asked.

"Yes. I've already met with one. Don't worry. I'll phone you up later from a different phone" I promised.

I was not comfortable speaking on this hotel phone any longer.

I remembered my attorney had instructed me not to talk to anyone about my case. Anything and everything I said would be used against me. Helicopters were flying over the hotel. In what seemed like just a moment in time, there was complete chaos. My whole life had changed. I had to phone home and break the news to my parents before they saw it in television. This kind of scandal would not be good for my legitimate talent manager mom who'd spent 25 years developing a reputable business that managed kids. My sister phoned immediately after catching it on TV.

"Jo, are you alright? I sat down to have some dinner and saw you on the 6 o'clock news! Is all of this true? Do you need anything? What can I do?" she asked concerned.

Even my family had not been aware of the double life I had been leading for so many years.

"Nothing, Sweetheart. Yes, it's true but I'll be fine" I said.

I didn't want to worry my family.

This had now become a high profile case, which meant perhaps I needed a different attorney who was experienced in these matters. Clearly, my problem was not just going to go away.

Finding the right attorney became a grueling process. I needed someone who could be a real 'pit bull" in court and fight for me. Gerry Scotti was a good choice. He had been a federal agent for years with DEA, and had left to practice criminal law. But not before helping to acquit legendary auto magnate John De Lorean on his alleged drug case. Gerry had operated on both sides of the law and knew how cops thought. He seemed like my guy.

"How much?" I asked him.

"This will cost you about $250,000" he said.

Things had definitely changed since my meeting with the previous attorney. By the time I met Gerri we had less than one day before my arraignment. I hired him. He briefed me as to what to expect in court the next day.

"They say there's going to be a lot of media there" he mentioned.

Always wary of being hit in the head by some crazy paparazzi trying to snap a shot with a huge camera, we felt I needed some help so two bodyguards were hired to escort me to court. My publicist felt he should be there too, to advise me. My courtroom entourage now included my attorney and his paralegal, two bodyguards, my boyfriend and my publicist; all of whom believed they should be with me.

We arrived at court at 7:30 am. Greeted by complete chaos there were so many photographers I couldn't see where I was going. The sheriff there had insisted on escorting me with an additional group of officers to insure my safety. Surrounded by an entire group of police officers there for my protection, I could barely place one foot successfully in front of the other to make my way through the madness. It seemed nothing could really shield me from the amount of media there determined to get their photo. Everyone was trying to get to me and I became scared of being trampled. Even one of my bodyguards got knocked in the head. A fight broke out as he lunged back at the huge camera that had hit him in the face. They insisted on taking me in through a private side entrance.

Once inside, the chaos continued. The courtroom was standing room only to a packed media audience and the cameras were everywhere. I listened as the judge read my charges aloud along with each count.

"Miss Gibson, you are being charged with 14 counts, 7 for pandering, 7 for pimping. You have a 15th count of conspiracy" he began.

I whispered in my attorney's ear.

"Oh my God, Gerri! And what's the conspiracy count for?" I asked.

"It's between you, your secretary Sherry, & the undercover cop."

"But I was my secretary Sherry!" I exclaimed.

"Don't worry. We'll handle it. You'll never do a day" he assured me.

Those would be famous last words…

My trial date was set. There would be at least nine months until my trial.

As time passed and my trial grew near, media fascination continued to grow. My parents were very worried about me. I was concerned about them too. Photographers were caught sending flowers with a hidden microphone planted in it to mom. Along with all the harassing phone calls she was receiving from journalists trying to get the story it was a difficult time for them too.

I remained in Arizona with my boyfriend. Fortunately, my animals had not been harmed during the police raid. But the news of my arrest had reached the small town we were hiding out in. It seemed a challenge to lay low and remain calm with my trial approaching. My business had now ceased to exist. Money was going out and nothing was coming in.

Joe had informed me that they would not be putting my record out. It seemed the distribution deal he had put together had fallen through with my arrest and they had backed out. I had created my escort service to assist in subsidizing costs for my recording career, and now my escort service was costing me my recording career.

It was a strange twist of fate.

One morning, I received a call from my attorney.

"I've got some interesting news" he began.

"Really? I could use some good news" I said.

"I was contacted by a gal named Natalie. She saw you on the news. Do you remember having met her as one of your girls?" he asked.

"Vaguely. What did she want?" I inquired curiously.

"She phoned me because apparently, the head investigating officer on your case contacted her with questions about whether she had been one of your girls. She informed them that she had met you but things never panned out and she never actually worked for you. At that point they told her that it didn't matter whether she really did work for you or not. They told her that if she did not cooperate and testify to what they wanted her to say, they would bring in the feds and prosecute her with tax evasion" he said.

"You're kidding me! How did they find her? What did she say?" I asked.

"She somehow knew enough to get off the phone with them and contact me. She's now your star witness" he said.

I could hear him smiling through the phone.

"They're going through your books they've got and contacting each girl. That's how they found her" he confirmed.

This was trouble. Each girl that cooperated in testifying against me represented a count. Each count held it's own sentence. The news had recently reported that the district attorney was trying to get me sentenced to 49 years. I flashed for a moment about my detective lover. Surely, he'd heard about all this. Where was he and what was he thinking? There was no safe way now to contact him without jeopardizing his safety. I remembered that they had my manuscript detailing my love affair with him and the immunity I had received. I was so glad I had not mentioned his name.

"There's one more thing" he added.

"What?"

"The Los Angeles Times received a copy of your manuscript from somebody working on the case. They're breaking the story about your affair with the detective and how you received immunity" he said.

The cops are the first ones to inform the papers about anything.

"On no! Do they know who he is? When are they breaking it?" I asked.

"It'll be in tomorrow's paper, front page. I've already received a copy called 'Babydol and the Officer'. They think they know who he is but they want you to confirm it."

"Why would I do that?" I asked.

"Well, Internal Affairs has contacted me. They say they'll go anywhere, any time to speak to you. They claim they're offering a deal" he said.

"Tell them no deal, Gerri. I'll never give him up" I confirmed.

"Are you sure? This could mean no jail time for you."

"No deal, Gerri" I said adamantly.

There was no way I would give him up. He had been my lover, my confidante, and my friend.

I hoped he would come to realize this after the story broke since there was no way I could reach him to reassure my loyalty.

"Ok, then. I'll tell them that. We'll line up Natalie as your witness. I'll call when I've got some more news. Hang in there" he said.

"Okay, Gerri. Thanks".

As the months passed leading up to my trial the media continued to hound me for an interview. I agreed to one or two with the understanding that I could only discuss my recording career. Every one that saw me on television might be a potential juror. I learned to play emotional dodge ball with investigative journalists as they tried to trap me into incriminating questions. There were a few however, who remained supportive and wished me good luck with my upcoming trial.

I was concerned about who they would find as my jury. Since my case was about sex, celebrities, and incredible amounts of money, would they even be able to find me an impartial jury of my peers? And who were my peers? Surely, the postal worker from UPS would not be considered impartial. What would he understand about my making $100,000 in a week and would he resent me for it?

Somehow, we got through the process and twelve jurors were chosen. The judge placed a gag order so no one was allowed to reveal any of the data in my black book and many of the big names were placed under court seal to shield them from media scrutiny. This would ultimately cause the LA Times to hire a fleet of attorneys after my trial was over to try to gain access to my black book with the high profile names.

But they were unsuccessful in getting it.

I had not been able to sleep much with the promise of trial just days away. Nightmares of the possibilities of being sent to prison haunted me at night. How would I survive that? I wasn't prepared for that kind of life nor well suited for it. Further, I had never been arrested before and knew nothing about it. Whom could I ask? I was a delicate feminine type not a common street fighter. My attorney was convinced that I would not be convicted but I had that terrible gut feeling again.

Just like the one I had before when I suspected that Robert and Candy were cops…

The prosecution was having difficulty getting the girls to actually show up in court to testify. Without their confession to the court there was no case against me. As long as the girls refused to show it was possible I might walk. My defense was entrapment. They had baited me in. Not the best defense but really the only one I had. My trial had begun and still, no girls. The judge spoke to the prosecuting attorney.

"You have until noon tomorrow to deliver your witnesses. If they are not here by then I'll have to dismiss the case" he ordered.

My attorney and I were elated. Was it possible that I might not go to prison after all? It was hard to believe that it had actually been six weeks since my trial had begun. Six weeks of the hell and uncertainty of my future. Perhaps everything would really be okay.

The following morning the circus continued. The count of conspiracy had now been dropped against me. The under-cover female officer I had met as Candy had been wired all along at our meetings. Everyone knew now that her name was Cynthia Neff. Her tapes were presented as evidence in court. The proud peacock of a district attorney had strutted around to show off playing the tapes.

"I have here exhibit # 72. They are tapes of Miss Gibson's secretary Sherry discussing business on the phone with the undercover officer. The conspiracy charge is between the three individuals who conspired to negotiate the deals of sex for money. They include; our undercover officer, Miss Gibson, and her secretary Sherry" he said.

There were a total of 129 exhibits of evidence retrieved from my belongings and used against me. Much of which were photos and letters from girls from all over the world writing with requests to work for my service. The tapes were played.

"Clearly, the voice of my client Miss Gibson and that of her secretary Sherry are one and the same. I move to strike the count of conspiracy as one cannot conspire against oneself" my attorney motioned.

Conspiracy requires a minimum of three people. The count was dropped.

But on this morning things were more critical. The judge had ordered that my girls show up by noon today or my case was dismissed. It was 11am and still no girls. I was nervous. It had been another difficult morning as they paraded me into court past the jury seated outside. They always bring the defendant in first. That was an odd moment. And now I was waiting for the outcome that would determine my fate. One more hour, and I might be free.

Then suddenly, at 11:45 the door flew open. In walked the girls. They were showing up to testify after all. My heart sank as I realized this sealed my fate. I was sure now that this would lead to my conviction and I would be sent to prison.

MY ARREST MAKES FRONT PAGE NEWS

Los Angel

ERNET: WWW.LATIMES.COM
ON: 1,098,347 DAILY / 1,385,787 SUNDAY

TUESDAY, SEPTEM
COPYRIGHT 1999 / THE TIMES MIRROR

CYION

B

ME

SDAY
TEMBER 14, 1999   CC

'Babydol' Alleges Affair With Officer

■ Crime: Police look into accused madam's claim a detective helped shield her from prosecution.

By CHUCK PHILIPS
TIMES STAFF WRITER

When authorities announced the arrest three months ago of Jody "Babydol" Gibson as one of Hollywood's leading madams, officials said they had seized a log book of her clients as well as a manuscript that details her life in the prostitution business.

What officials did not mention, however, was that the book proposal written by Gibson alleges that she had an affair with a Beverly Hills police detective who was investigating her escort business. In the manuscript—a key section of which Los Angeles police say they have not seen—Gibson contends that the relationship played a crucial role in shielding her from prosecution during earlier investigations, sources said.

Describing the affair, which
Please see BOOK, B3

Associated Press

Jody "Babydol" Gibson

LA TIMES BREAKS STORY OF MY DETECTIVE LOVER

240

Chapter 30: Prison

"We the jury find the defendant Jody Babydol Gibson guilty of the charge of pimping".

Those words would echo in my mind for close to the next three years. Right then and there, the bailiff in court carted me off after the verdict came in. It had actually been a hung jury for nine of the ten days allowed before declaring a mistrial. I had been convicted on three counts of the fifteen counts against me. The conspiracy charge had been dropped early in the case, and all seven counts of pandering completely dismissed because the three girls out of the seven that actually showed up all testified that it was indeed they who approached me, not I who solicited them for employment with my escort service. Four of the girls simply refused to show up at all so those four counts were dismissed. That left the remaining three charges of pimping.

The judge sentenced me to a total of three years to run concurrent instead of consecutively, which would have been considerably worse at a total of nine years. As this was the judge's first high profile superior court case (he had been merely a municipal judge prior to this), there seemed to be a large amount of 'political agenda' which began to surround the scenario;

1) The original judge who had initially been assigned the case was an older gentleman who'd been on the bench for 30 years, rumored to be a decent and fair judge. However, on the day trial was to first begin he was mysteriously removed from my case and replaced with a young Municipal Judge who had never tried a Superior Court case before.

2) My bail, which at been at $25,000 all year, had been raised to an unreasonable and exorbitant amount for my appeal bond to $500,000! (Heidi Fleiss' appeal bond had gone from the same $25,000 to only $100,000, and hers included added charges of drugs and money laundering)

3) After coming up with the $500,000 for the Appeal Bond which would allow me to remain out on bail to fight my appeal, and was my legal right, the judge then completely denied me my legal right to it and insisted I be taken into custody and sent straight to state prison.

4) With no prior convictions of any kind we were told that I would be sent to a minimum security facility, more like a 'camp for first timers.' Instead, I was sent to the most severe prison in the state of California; a Level 4- Maximum security facility known as Chowchilla (nicknamed Chowkilla) the only facility for women that houses Death Row inmates.

The charges associated with state prison are; murder, conspiracy for murder, kidnapping, grand theft auto, car jacking (which serves a life sentence) and my charge. I was handcuffed from my wrist to my waist on a chain of 30 girls, and with my feet shackled, I was sent to the most severe prison in the state of California.

So, this was what I had to look forward too.

My journey through prison was the darkest and loneliest road I shall ever walk in this lifetime. I was constantly in a state of confusion trying to survive in a world so foreign to me. My first night in jail awaiting my transfer to prison was a horror.

Prison would be an endless series of horrors that I would come to know. Frequent strip searches, which included bending over to reach your ankles, while an ugly female butch guard spread your ass and looked up your asshole with a flashlight would be just the beginning.

"We know who you are, Gibson. You and your Hollywood celebrity life! This is our crib now and you're gonna do exactly what we say" the ugly female butch guard instructed.

Then, they brought out a scissors and proceeded to cut off all my hair. I cried so hard while they cut that my eyes were swollen shut.

"Ha! Wait until the prison gynecologist gets a hold of you!" she laughed.

She really seemed to be enjoying all of this.

A fate worse than death, I then found myself at the hands of this maniac prison doctor who rams his hand up your pussy while his wife stands there watching. I tried to make conversation with her in the hopes of gaining some sympathy. When that didn't work, I said that I had my period and somehow managed to escape the moment. A TB shot, your mug shot taken, and then back to the cell with the 30 girls to see what horrors befall you next. Nobody will tell you anything either. If you try to ask a question you're told to "sit down and shut up". And if you argue or refuse to comply you get a 'write-up', which includes having additional time added on to your sentence.

There is no way to use the phone for the first eight weeks there either. No way to call loved ones to notify them to let them know you're still alive. The only way around that one is to try to get a job as a clerk, or sweeping and cleaning as a porter. And since all five thousand women on the yard want a job so that they could make that sacred phone call home, the line started to the left. But somehow, I was able to get a job as a clerk. Apparently, my case was playing out on the only television there and the handsome male guard recognized me. Even with all my hair chopped off.

I found out later that after I did get to use the phone to call home, inmates spying caught the number and had called my home too, terrorizing my family with threats to kill me by the following day unless money was sent to them.

"Damn, Babydol, you look all tore up compared to how you look on television!" the inmates would say.

No kidding. I learned to ignore it. My case was all about sex, money, and Hollywood and they never let me forget it. I was a complete target with all the inmates badgering me daily for money, or to 'hook them up' with phone numbers or whatever. They never left me alone and life became a constant game of emotional dodge ball just to make it through the day. Daily dialogue consisted of "Fuck, Bitch, or Ho" and the screaming, fighting, and all the noise made you long for just five minutes of peace. Their tales of shooting heroin, murder, or stealing became common conversation and with eight girls to a room all serving life sentences for murder, violence was a way of life with them. One girl had threatened to mar my face with acid.

Another time I was jumped by three girls and locked in a room and beaten losing many of my front teeth, before being rushed to the prison doctor with two black eyes and a concussion in my head.

"Stop hitting me" I screamed.

I flew up in the air and the next thing I knew I landed on the floor, before jumping back up. Three girls, one of whom was three times my size was punching me in the face!.

Oh, God, please don't let her break my nose, and leave me at the hands of the prison jailhouse doctor! I could feel myself swallowing parts of my teeth.

My educated formal English, drug illiterate history, and refined manners made me stick out like a sore thumb. Prison was their turf and I was the odd one.

There was no logical reason to support my being sent to such a severe prison. I had never been arrested before and this was not considered a heinous crime. It paled in comparison to the charges of my fellow inmates most of whom were there for murder. This was a world so violent that anger, hatred, and despair all united to form Satan in the faces of people disguised as women.

Ultimately, the challenges of contaminated drinking water, bad food, being surrounded by disease, combined with the stress of violence, hatred, and fighting for one's life daily, would chip away at my vegetarian perfect health;

I would become so ill with the intended lack of poor medical attention after being refused common antibiotics, that I would find myself rushed by ambulance in the middle of the night to the hospital with double pneumonia and staphylococcus in my lungs. Losing 50% of my lung capacity and barely able to breathe, I would remain in a hospital bed past my scheduled release date for six weeks. Near death upon my release at 85 pounds and unable to walk, it would take almost a year to regain my health.

So, why had I been sent there? My family had been informed that I would be taken to a minimum-security facility, much like a camp. But for some reason, no one was able to offer any explanation for this. We were all sure it was the politics surrounding my case. The following sub chapters outline just a few of my experiences:

a) Yes, There Are Lesbians in Prison

Homosexuality is alive and well and flourishing behind the prison walls. Although I was a liberal with a 'live and let live' attitude, I was a heterosexual with minor experiences indulging in bisexual behavior. Besides, even if I were gay these gals were definitely not my type. Many were just like men referred to as "stud broads". Some managed to grow hair on their chin like a light beard. With matching hairy armpits, many chose to emulate a construction worker look complete with big hanging belly over jeans and sleeveless tee shirts. They spit, cursed, fought, and acted just like men. Size was everything so the bigger you were, the more you ruled. They assigned each other masculine and feminine roles with the masculine ones taking possession of the more feminine ones with violence and sex. If you were someone's bitch, this meant that you were owned by one of the masculine stud broads. Interference of any kind would result in extremely possessive and jealous behavior, which might likely get you killed. I once saw a girl get boiling hot water thrown at her for simply smiling at another girl's bitch, leaving her in the prison hospital for weeks to nurse her third degree burns.

Often, one could see them sitting together embraced in a romantic embrace with arms wrapped around each other passionately making out. If you were placed in a room with two girls that were lovers, you would constantly hear them eating each other's pussy. Sometimes, they would order you out of the room while they had their sex sessions. There were eight girls to a room so a full room would lead them to continue their sex action in the shower. The showers were open from the neck up and the knees down so there was never a private moment. That made masturbation out of the question. Even though I was a heterosexual who preferred the company of men, all the slurping, sucking, and cum sounds began to turn me on. Many girls approached me with a request to 'do my time with them' which meant they wanted to couple up with me. It was not easy being completely cut off from intimacy and sex for close to three years but I did my time alone. I would constantly have anxiety attacks, which created the challenge of finding ways to channel all the frustrated sexual energy.

Some girls were 'gay for the stay' which meant that outside of prison they led heterosexual lives with husbands and boyfriends. But inside, they were just as passionate with a woman as they would be with a man. They would forever make referrals to their pussy too like "my pussy's sweet" and "your pussy isn't".

There were often subtle acts as well like braiding each other's hair often leading to styles known as cornrow. This was considered an endearing act almost like flirting so, if a girl asked to braid your hair that meant she liked you. One had to handle these moments delicately too, so as not to anger another by making her feel rejected. I found that the best way to offset this was to say that I was waiting for my man on the outside.

Needless to say this was just one of the many challenges of prison.

b) It's Not On the List

Every three months in state prison one was allowed to receive a quarterly "box". This included a list of personal items sent from home that met prison specifications i.e.; a personal hairbrush, or purchased items, which were searched thoroughly and approved by state prison guards. The criteria for this was incredibly specific right down to certain colors, shades of shampoo bottles, and sizes or amounts. Creams and shampoos were only accepted in clear plastic bottles. I actually paid a girl $13 for a 59 cent bottle of hydrogen peroxide that she smuggled out of the prison hospital so I could keep my hair it's lightest shade of blonde by putting it on and applying a blow dryer. (What price beauty?) One got so tired of feeling unattractive it forced you to go to great lengths just to feel a little bit pretty. Limited clothing items were restricted with no colors like green, grey, or brown, as they resembled colors worn by prison staff. No writing on clothing or raised embossed lettering was accepted.

Television sets were allowed in sizes 5" to 9", along with radios, CD players, or a boom box. The size of the quarterly box also had to meet specific size and weight. If it was even one ounce over the criteria, it was refused and sent back forcing you to wait another four months until the next time. It didn't matter if your 80 yr. old grandmother had spent a month to try to get everything together for you. If it didn't meet the criteria it was refused. A towel sent could not be too thick or too pretty so as not to make the other inmates jealous, lest they kill you for it. My sister worked so hard running around for weeks making sure everything was right just so that I might get that nice fluffy towel I liked that she cried to me on the phone after sending it.

The grueling process used to receive this precious box began at 5 am. You were given notice to report to a prison location wherein you were placed in a cold cell for up to eight hours until your name was called. You prayed that some mean and ugly butch prison guard wasn't on duty for the search that day, lest she sent something back just for the hell of it because she didn't like your look. The entire contents of the box was searched and documented and then placed in a large clear plastic bag which you were forced to carry all the way back to your yard.

The distance for the walk back to your yard was approximately half a mile so if you were fortunate enough to be sent a television or a boom box, you had to carry it all the way back regardless of how heavy it was. If you couldn't carry it you couldn't keep it. So, believe me you found a way to carry it.

Once back in your room you would find the other eight girls searching through your new possessions, threatening your life because they liked that new towel your family took such precious time to choose for you. Or perhaps they wanted that radio you couldn't wait to hear your favorite CD on. The other less fortunate inmates that had no one on the outside who cared for them got to be reminded for just a little while of what it feels like to have someone by going through yours. So, you learned to share.

To the other girls in the room the status of receiving that precious box meant that someone on the outside cared about you. Enough to go through all that just to try to remind you that you were still loved while you were completely cut off from the outside world, family, and friends.

Even if what they sent was not on the list…

c) Loneliness and Deprivation

When you are incarcerated you are virtually consumed by loneliness while being completely cut off from family, friends, freedom, and life itself. Mail takes weeks to go out and weeks to receive. A simple phone call is restricted to fifteen minutes, which you must sign up for in the morning, and wait on a long line for hours for later that afternoon. Your freedom has been stripped from you as you are told when to get up, when to sleep, when to eat, when to work.

There is never a private moment to release your grief and one must never cry or let others see your tears as they are considered a sign of weakness. And the weak do not survive. At one point I was so lonely that I cut out pictures of animals from magazines and pasted them on my wall with toothpaste as glue, just to think they were my friends.

The concept of prison life rests on the deprivation of the inmate. The inmate is to have nothing and learn to exist without. You receive a minimum amount of state issued clothing and if it should be lost or stolen it cannot be replaced. One pair of sneakers for two years and you better keep them clean lest the others harass you for having dirty ones.

It's always cold with its grey brick walls because they keep the air conditioning on even through the winter. I learned to keep warm by placing hot water in an empty shampoo bottle and sleeping with it in my bed.

In my room there were girls who were doing life sentences and had been inside prison for 18 years. One of them is named Wanda and she complains about a piece of thread found in the shower that she says is from someone's assigned state panties. She blames me and begins to argue. I insist they're not mine because I don't wear state panties anymore since my sister sent me store bought ones from home that I received in my box. Determined to take out her anger and grief out on someone, Wanda picks up the bottles of acid and threatens to disfigure my face with it. She's pretty strong physically, and has a lot of influence with the other lifers there.

"Bitch, this is a thread from your damn state panties! I found it in the shower! Now, I'm gonna fuck you up!" Wanda threatened.

She was doing a life sentence for murder and was never going home. Killing me meant nothing to her and she felt she could get away with anything.

"I don't wear state panties since my sister sent me some in my box" I said.

"I know it's yours, bitch. I'm gonna pour these chemicals all over your face" she threatened.

The other six girls in the room sat there and did nothing. The doors in the cell were locked and only opened for five minutes once every hour. The glass windows were soundproof so the guards outside wouldn't have to hear all the noise. There was no one to call, and no one to help me. The whole thing seemed utterly ridiculous to me, anyway. We were arguing about a thread from a panty in a room full of girls? Was she nuts? There was nothing left to do but try to negotiate.

"Hey, Wanda. How 'bout I give you those new playing cards my sister sent me? I haven't even used them yet. I'll even throw in my pretty new towel" I bargained.

I tried to remain quiet and calm since any altercation would result in added time on my sentence and keep my mind on the big picture, which was getting out. The other lifers know this and try to "take your days" by getting your sentenced time increased. This helps ease their anguish.

That seemed to work and that's how it was. There was no manual for you to read on how to get through all this insanity. You were completely on your own and it was an ugly madness.

Another day in hell and I'm still in here. I can feel the evil that surrounds me. Can't complain to anyone or they'll kill you. I've got to sign up for the phone today to hear my sister's voice. I begin to forget who I am as I melt into the daily grind of robotic prison existence. There's a long line for the phone but I don't care. I have to hear her voice or I'll die. It's the only thing that reminds me I'm still alive. I begin to forget who I am and that I have a life on the outside. My sister and her strength remind me. I begin to wonder; will anyone remember me when I finally get out of here? Will I get out of here? What if they try to find some illegal loophole to keep me in this hell a bit longer?

Finally, it's my turn to use the phone. I call home praying to hear my sister's voice. She answers. I'm so grateful to hear her. She keeps telling me that I'm going to get out and that one day soon this will all be over. I start to cry silently so no one sees me. She promises that I'll see the sun and the beautiful sky and the world will look beautiful to me again.

One day...

Towards the end of my stay in prison I begin to get a cough, which lasts for weeks, but they don't care and the prison guard still puts me to work outside in the freezing cold. After a trip to the prison doctor I am refused a simple antibiotic and told that it won't help anyway. My fever increases to 102 and I insist that an antibiotic will help prevent this from getting worse. I am denied. My health begins to deteriorate so that I do not believe I will make it to my release in three weeks. I explain that I have always led a healthy lifestyle free of drugs, smoking, or alcohol, and that I know what I need.

A trip to the prison library leads me to search for any medical books to tell me what I have, but I find none there. I am denied the antibiotics again and become so sick and weak that I can no longer make the walk across the street to the chow hall to eat. My body begins to deteriorate more and I have difficulty breathing.

The inmates who had befriended me witness all this and begin to try to help my condition by offering me their asthma inhalers to help me breathe. But nothing works.

Until one night at 2am I awake to find that I am no longer able to breathe at all. I am rushed by ambulance to the hospital.

Glad to be receiving some kind of health care, I am diagnosed and told that each of my lungs has it's own private pneumonia, along with staphylococcus. They tell me there are only three drugs in the world that are strong enough to conquer this and that my body is resistant to two of them. The one remaining is the strongest of the three, and is referred to by doctors as "the big gun". My condition is so serious that they IV a pick straight to the Aorta in my heart and the big gun shoots through my veins for three weeks. This drug is so strong that it kills the bacteria and pneumonia in my lungs but rapes my body of the nutrients it requires to gain my health back.

I now begin to get fevers of 104. They place me on slabs of ice every few hours to try to bring the fever down. They refuse to let me sleep for more than an hour and wake me frequently for fear that the high fever will leave me brain dead during sleep. The slabs of ice I'm forced to lie on lead to a severe chill, which does not go away.

I lose the use of my legs, unable to walk because of the Neuropathy, which results from being in a hospital bed sedentary for too long. My release date from prison finally arrives to find me too sick to be released. I now become the property of the hospital, which refuses to release me.

"I'm gonna die right here in this hospital bed aren't I doctor?"

He doesn't answer me.

My family is notified that they should come to see me since I might not make it. I am down to 85 pounds. My mom and sister fly in to witness this horror, leaving my dad behind who's too sick to make the long trip up north. Upon seeing my atrophied condition, my sister insists on taking me home to heal. The hospital insists that I am their property.

"I am going in there and taking my sister home. You sign these papers now!" she demanded.

Not without a fight, she talks them into releasing me to her as she is 'next of kin. I am wheeled out in a wheel chair with masks on my face, too fragile physically to face the air outside.

My sister carries me up two flights of stairs because I cannot walk.

But I am home…

Chapter 31: Epilogue: "Life Lessons"

Although this journey was more horrible than you can imagine I took from it valuable life lessons;

a) THE LAW and PROSTITUTION

I will never believe that prostitution is a criminal act that warrants a prison sentence. Immoral, to some perhaps, and certainly not right for everyone; but not criminal. When there are two consenting adults there is no victim.

This is an antiquated law in dire need of change.

50 years ago, if a black man spoke back to a white man he was put in jail. And if a doctor performed an abortion on a woman even if a rape had taken place, he was sent to jail.

On the day I was being sentenced I was allowed to speak. I wanted to ask the judge this question; if I'd have introduced a girl to a guy, and instead of him handing her a $1000, he took her shopping. While there I requested she pick me up a pair of $400 shoes (my cut on $1000). Would I still be going to state prison? My lawyer strongly advised me to say nothing as I was being sentenced.

Where do we draw the line? A sugar daddy that gives a girl an allowance? A woman that marries a much older man for financial security? Are these acts illegal too? Where lies the difference?

Interestingly enough, was the fact that there were no victims as my incarceration proved. Every inmate convicted of a state crime must pay what's called "restitution" to the victims and their families regardless of the nature of their crime. The amount can vary from $100 to $1,000,000 and every inmate has to do this. But, in my case THERE WAS NO RESTITUTION. Why? Because there were NO VICTIMS.

Change comes about when people of the same mind and thought unite together to bring upon the change. Peacefully, although changing the law is not an easy task.

That said, the law is still the law and I have learned to respect it. Until the law is changed we must respect the law for without it there would be chaos.

Fortunately, we live in a free country like United States of America where at least we have a chance to speak our mind to bring about change.

b) COMPASSION for the DYSFUNCTION of OTHERS

Compassion for the dysfunction of others for whom life has given an unfortunate beginning. With the breakdown of the family unit young girls are having babies with three different daddies before age 20. The single parent is struggling and cannot be there to raise their children properly. Stealing, crime, and drugs become the way out. The alcoholic parents instill their abuse and negative programming and the vicious cycle continues as their kids repeat the only behavior they've come to know. The lucky ones may realize this halfway through their adult life while the others never do.

So have compassion for others that life has given a bad beginning for they really have no clue.

c) ALWAYS TRUST YOUR GUT INTSTINCT

Instinct is the language of the soul. It is the subconscious mind that knows all, breaking through to communicate with the conscious mind. Ever have that gut feeling that you should or shouldn't have done something? That is gut instinct and we all have it. The one time I ignored it led me to a meeting, which led to my arrest.

Always trust your gut instinct for it's there to guide you even when the intellect cannot.

d) EVERYBODY is DOING EVERYTHING

So wake up and smell the coffee. Many of the people preaching their gospels are the biggest hypocrites of all. The very men that are sending people to jail are guilty of illegal acts themselves.

Most of the congressmen in our senate have no idea what's in the very bills they pass or deny.

Don't be naïve enough to think that everyone is looking out for you and has your best interest at heart. Learn to look out for yourself.

During my incarceration I witnessed many examples of hypocrisy and wastes of money at taxpayer's expense. For example, something called "a dry run" in which an inmate who has no court date is removed and sent through the grueling motions of a day in court which begins with being awakened at 1am. You are then placed in a freezing cold cell with just a bench and a roll of toilet paper to rest your head on for up to eight hours until transportation arrives to take you to the court date you insisted you did not have to begin with. Shackled from wrist to waist and ankles, you are then taken and placed into another freezing cold cell for the remainder of the court day. At the end of the day, you are transported back to your own cell but not without being "reprocessed" back into the court system which must happen every time an inmate leaves a facility. This process generally takes up to 10 hours so maybe you return to your bed 30 grueling hours later, all the while reminding anyone who'll listen that you confirmed you did not have court that day to begin with.

All this just so the marshals can make money, since every time an inmate is transferred the marshals get paid. And that's just one example of misuse in our penal system

It's important to find something you can believe in. But don't be in denial about the facts because at the end of the day, everybody is doing everything. Be aware.

e) THOUGHT IS REALITY; MANIFEST YOUR DREAMS

If you can see it, you can be it. Everything begins with the thoughts in your mind. They create your reality. No one has a crystal ball to tell you that you can't accomplish your dreams. You can manifest that which you want and the possibilities are endless so never let anyone prevent you from chasing your dreams. We each live in our own sense of reality created from that that begins in our mind and we can change that reality as well.

Every word you utter is an affirmation in the universe.

So learn to recognize the thoughts in your mind. You control your thoughts; they do not control you.

f) BE CAREFUL WHAT YOU WISH FOR

You might get it, but not necessarily in the package you thought; I wished for fame and fortune and I got it; but not at all in the way I expected it...

g) HUMILITY

Is important because just when you think you know

everything, you find out that you know nothing at all.

h) SURVIVAL

And most importantly regardless of how difficult the struggle and no matter how bad things seem, or just when you think you simply can't go on any longer, I am living proof that you can survive.

Printed in the United States
71948LV00003B/85-93